BIBLIOGRAPHIA   JAMAICENSIS

BIBLIOGRAPHIA JAMAICENSIS

A LIST OF JAMAICA BOOKS AND PAMPHLETS,
MAGAZINE ARTICLES, NEWSPAPERS,
AND MAPS, MOST OF WHICH
ARE IN THE LIBRARY
OF THE INSTITUTE
OF JAMAICA

BY FRANK CUNDALL

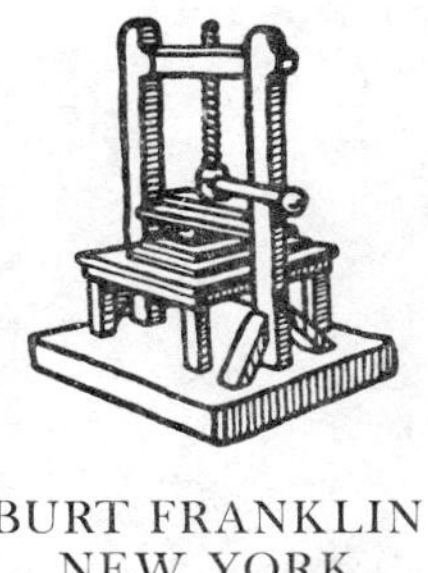

BURT FRANKLIN
NEW YORK

Published by LENOX HILL Pub. & Dist. Co. (Burt Franklin)
235 East 44th St., New York, N.Y. 10017
Originally Published: 1902
Reprinted: 1971
Printed in the U.S.A.

S.B.N.: 8337-0740X
Library of Congress Card Catalog No.: 70-168276
Burt Franklin: Bibliography and Reference Series 433
American Classics in History and Social Science 206

Reprinted from the original edition in the University of Pennsylvania
Library.

CONTENTS

CROSS-REFERENCES.

BOOKS.

PREFACE.

THE following is a list of Jamaica books and pamphlets, newspapers and maps, most of which are represented in the library of the Institute of Jamaica : the titles of those absent from its shelves are prefixed by an *.

It need hardly be added that copies of works not represented will be gladly received by the Institute ; and that the titles of any books or pamphlets unrecorded will also be welcomed

The books have been classified under the various headings suggested by the works themselves, as well as by a study of Jamaica History.

The list was originally compiled for insertion in the " Jamaica Handbook'' for 1902. For the sake of space the titles were in some instances shortened, and the sizes of the volumes and other bibliographical information omitted. But, even when compressed as much as possible, the list was found too long for insertion in the Handbook; and it is accordingly issued in its present form.

A few notes of general cross-reference have been added to the classification, but complete cross-references would be more voluminous than the list itself.

All books treating on the West Indies generally could of course be fairly included in a Jamaica Bibliography, but, as this would have unduly swelled the list, it has been thought advisable to include only such West Indian books as deal with Jamaica alone, adding only a few of the principal of those which deal chiefly with this island. All books and pamphlets dealing solely with Jamaica have been catalogued, without reference to merit.

The following list is, therefore, really rather a series of notes for a bibliography of Jamaica than a complete bibliography itself. It is, perhaps, as a bibliography most incomplete with respect to botany, for which reference should be made to Urban's " Symbolae Antillanae."

The works are arranged, under their severa headings, in chronological order. Strict chronology has, however, been departed from in certain cases, in order to place subsequent editions with the first issues of various works.

Magazine articles which have been reprinted in pamphlet form have, in common with pamphlets originally published as such, been treated as pamphlets, and classified with the books. Those which have not been reprinted are placed together under Magazine Articles.

An index of names of authors and subjects of biographical notices will be found at the end.

F. C.

Kingston, Jamaica,
 October, 1902.

BOOKS.

eertijds in 't Spaans beschreeven door den Heer Antonius de Herrera. . . . . *Leyden,*   1707

9—THE STORY OF THE LIFE OF COLUMBUS AND THE DISCOVERY OF JAMAICA. By Frank Cundall, F.S.A. *Kingston,*   1894

10—ABORIGINAL INDIAN REMAINS IN JAMAICA. By J. E. Duerden, A.R.C.Sc. (Lond.) : with a "Note on the Craniology of the Aborigines of Jamaica" by Professor A. C. Haddon, M.A., D.Sc. *Kingston,* 1897

II. ii. CAPTURE AND SETTLEMENT.

11—A BRIEF AND PERFECT JOURNAL of the late Proceedings and Successe of the English Army in the West Indies. Continued until June the 24th, 1655, together with some quæres inserted and answered. Published for satisfaction of all such who desire truly to be informed in these particulars. By I. S., an Eye-witnesse. *London,*   1655

11a— A BOOK OF THE CONTINUATION OF FOREIGN PASSAGES. . . . . Moreover, an attempt on the Island of Jamaica, and Taking the Town of St. Jago de la Viga, beating the Enemy from their forts and ordnance, being a body of 3,000 men, and so took possession of the Island, May 10, 1655. With a full Description thereof. . . *London,* 1657

12—ANOTHER CRY of the Innocent and Oppressed for Justice, or a third relation of the unjust proceedings at the Sessions held . . . for the County of Middlesex and . . . . for the City of London, ... in the year 1664, with and against 45 of the people of God whom the world in scorn calls Quakers of which 39 were sentenced, for a pretended breach of the late Act, 34 of which to be transported to the island of Gamaica, for the space of seven years, and five to Bridewel. . . .   Printed in 1665

13—NAMES OF THE PRINCIPAL PLANTERS AND SETTLERS IN JAMAICA. 1633 [sic. ? 1663]. (From a MS. of Charles Long, Esq.) ; and Assemblies and Councils in Jamaica, (from a MS. history written by Dr. Barham). Reprint of the Middle Hill private press,   [? 1840]

14—THE NARRATIVE OF GENERAL VENABLES ; with an appendix of papers relating to the Expedition to the West Indies and the Conquest of Jamaica 1654-1655. Edited for the Royal Historical Society by C. H. Firth. *London,*   1900

II. iii.   SLAVERY AND EMANCIPATION.

15—* AN ACCOUNT OF THE NUMBER OF NEGROES delivered into the islands of Barbados, Jamaica and Antego from . . 1698 to 1708.   [? 1710]

17—AN ARGUMENT in the case of James Sommersett a negro, wherein it is attempted to demonstrate the present unlawfulness of domestic slavery in England. To which is prefixed a state of the case. By Mr. Hargrave, one of the Counsel for the Negro. 2nd. ed. *London,* 1775

18—OBSERVATIONS UPON THE AFRICAN SLAVE TRADE and on the situation of the Negroes in the West Indies, with some proposed regulations for a more mild and Human Treatment of them. By a Jamaica Planter. *London,*   1788

19—REMARKS UPON THE SITUATION OF NEGROES in Jamaica, impartially made from a local experience of nearly thirteen years in that island. By W[illiam] Beckford, jnr., formerly of Somerly in Suffolk, and late of Hertford in Jamaica. *London,*   1788

20—* AN ACCOUNT OF THE ISLAND OF JAMAICA, with Reflections on the treatment, occupation and provisions of the Slaves, &c.   *Newcastle,*   1788

21—AN ANSWER TO THE REV. MR. CLARKSON'S Essay on the Slavery and Commerce of the Human Species, particularly the African ; in a series of letters from a gentleman in Jamaica to his friend in London, wherein many of the mistakes and misrepresentations of Mr. Clarkson are pointed out, both with regard to the manner in which that Commerce is carried on in Africa and the Treatment of the Slaves in the West Indies. Showing at the same time the Antiquity, Universality and Lawfulness of Slavery as ever having been one of the States and Condition of Mankind.. By G. Francklyn. *London,* 1789

22—TWO REPORTS F OM THE COMMITTEE OF THE HONOURABLE HOUSE OF ASSEMBLY of Jamaica, appointed to examine into, and report to the House, the Allegations and Charges contained in the several Petitions which have been presented to the British House of Commons, on the subject of the Slave Trade, and the treatment of the Negroes, &c. *London,* 1789

23—NOTES ON THE TWO REPORTS from the Committee of the Honourable House of Assembly of Jamaica, appointed to examine into, and to report to the House, the Allegations and Charges contained in the several Petitions which have been presented to the British House of Commons on the subject of the Slave Trade and the Treatment of the Negroes. By a Jamaica Planter. *London,* 1789

24—A SPEECH delivered at a Free Conference between the Honourable the Council and Assemby of Jamaica, held on the 19th Nov., 1789 on the subject of Mr. Wilberforce's propositions in the House of Commons concerning the Slave Trade. By Bryan Edwards. *Kingston,* 1789

The same. London, 1790

25—REPORT, RESOLUTIONS AND REMONSTRANCE of the Honourable the Council and Assembly of Jamaica, at a joint Committee, on the subject of the Slave-Trade, in a session which began the 20th of October, 1789 . . . *London,* 1790

26—*Proceedings of the House of the Assembly of Jamaica, on the Sugar and Slave Trade. 1793

27—AN ACCOUNT OF THE EMANCIPATION of the Slaves of Unity Valley Pen, in Jamaica. By David Barclay. *London,* 1801

*The same. 2nd ed.

28—THE REPORT FROM A COMMITTEE OF THE HOUSE OF ASSEMBLY of Jamaica, appointed in a session, which began on the 23rd of October, 1804, to inquire into the Proceedings of the Imperial Parliament of Great Britain and Ireland relative to the Slave Trade. *London,* 1805

29—AN ESSAY CONCERNING SLAVERY and the danger Jamaica is expos'd to from the too great number of Slaves, and the too little care that is taken to manage them, and a proposal to prevent the further importation of negroes into that Island. *London,* n. d. [before 1807]

30—NEGRO EMANCIPATION MADE EASY; with reflections on the African Institution and Slave Registry Bill. By a British Planter [of Jamaica]. [*London*], 1816

31—A LETTER TO THE MEMBERS OF THE IMPERIAL PARLIAMENT, referring to the evidence contained in the proceedings of the House of Assembly of Jamaica, and shewing the injurious and unconstitutional tendency of the proposed Slave Registry Bill. By a Colonist. *London,* 1816

32—NEGRO SLAVERY: or a view of some of the more prominent features of that state of society, as it exists in the United States of America and in the Colonies of the West Indies, especially in Jamaica. [By R. Taylor]. *London,* 1823

33—JAMAICA PLANTER'S GUIDE: or a system of planting and managing a Sugar Estate in that island and throughout the British West Indies in general. By Thomas Roughley. *London,* 1823

34—AN ADDRESS to the Right Hon. Geo. Canning on the Present State of this Island [Jamaica] and other matters. By Dennis Reid of the parish of Westmoreland. *Jamaica,* 1823

35—A VOICE FROM JAMAICA; in reply to William Wilberforce, Esq., M. P. By Rev. George Wilson Bridges, B. A. *London,* 1823
The same. 2nd ed. 1823
The same. 3rd. ed.
The same. 4th ed. 1824

36—PLAIN FACTS, or circumstances as they really are: being an impartial and unprejudiced account of the State of the Black Population in the island of Jamaica. By Nathaniel Sotham. *London,* 1824

37—FACTS ILLUSTRATIVE of the condition of the Negro Slaves in Jamaica; with notes and an appendix. By Thomas Cooper. *London,* 1824

38—FACTS VERIFIED UPON OATH, in contradiction of the Report of the Rev. Thomas Cooper, concerning the general condition of the Slaves in Jamaica: and more especially relative to the management and treatment of the Slaves upon Georgia Estate, in the Parish of Hanover in that island. [By R. Hibbert]. *London,* 1824

39—A LETTER TO ROBERT HIBBERT, Jun. Esq., in reply to his pamphlet entitled " Facts verified upon oath in contradiction of the Report of the Rev. Thomas Cooper concerning the general condition of the Slaves in Jamaica." To which are added a Letter from Mrs. Cooper to R. Hibbert, jnr., Esq. and an appendix containing an exposure of the falsehoods and calumnies of that gentlemen's affidavitmen. By Thomas Cooper. *London,* 1824

40—STATE OF SOCIETY AND SLAVERY IN JAMAICA [By Britannicus, a member of the House of Assembly of Jamaica] in a Reply to an article in the Edinburgh Review No. LXXV. *London,* 1824

41—CORRESPONDENCE BETWEEN GEORGE HIBBERT, ESQ., AND THE REV. T. COOPER, relative to the condition of the Negro Slaves in Jamaica, extracted from the Morning Chronicle ; also a Libel on the character of Mr. and Mrs. Cooper, published in 1823, in several of the Jamaica Journals ; with notes and remarks. By Thomas Cooper. *London,* 1824.

42—THE REV. MR. COOPER AND HIS CALUMNIES against Jamaica, particularly his late Pamphlet in reply to Facts Verified on Oath. By a West Indian. *Jamaica,* 1825

43—A VIEW OF SLAVERY in connection with Christianity : being the substance of a Discourse delivered in the Wesleyan Chapel, Stoney Hill, Jamaica, Sep. 19, 1824, by Robert Young, Wesleyan Missionary. With an Appendix containing the Resolutions of the Missionaries in that connection at a general meeting held in Kingston Sep 6, 1824. (*Jamaica* 1824.) *London* reprinted, 1825

44—THE WEST INDIES AS THEY ARE, or a real picture of slavery but more particularly as it exists in Jamaica. By Rev. R. Bickell. In three parts with notes. *London,* 1825

45—NOTES ON THE PRESENT CONDITION of the Negroes in Jamaica, By H[enry] T[homas] De la Beche, F. R. S. *London,* 1825
The same. 1826

46—NOTES IN DEFENCE OF THE COLONIES on the increase and decrease of the Slave population of the British West Indies. By a West Indian. *Jamaica,* 1826

47—AN APPEAL TO THE CHRISTIAN PHILANTHROPY of the people of Great Britain and Ireland, in behalf of the Religious instruction and Conversion of three hundred thousand Negro Slaves. By the Rev. J. M. Trew, Rector of the Parish of St. Thomas-in-the-East, in the island of Jamaica. *London,* 1826

48—A PRACTICAL VIEW of the present state of slavery in the West Indies, or an examination of Mr. Stephen's " Slavery of the British West Indian Colonies" containing more particularly an account of the actual condition of the negroes of Jamaica . . . also strictures on the Edinburgh Review and on the Pamphlets of Mr. Cooper and Mr. Bickell. By Alexander Barclay. *London,* 1826
The same. 2nd ed., with additions. *London,* 1828
The same. 3rd ed. 1828

49—NEGRO EMANCIPATION no Philanthropy, a letter to the Duke of Wellington by a Jamaica Landed Proprietor. *London,* 1830

50—A LETTER TO THE RIGHT HONORABLE THE EARL OF SUFFIELD on subjects connected with Slavery in the island of Jamaica ; with an abstract of the Law now in force in that colony, for the Government of Slaves. By Andrew Graham Dignum. . . . *London,* 1832

51—Return of Slaves, Jamaica. 1832

52—*Speeches of Mr. Barrett and Mr. Burge at a meeting of Planters, merchants and others interested in the West India Colonies, on Slavery in Jamaica, *London,* 1833

53—Evidence upon Oath touching the condition and treatment of the Negro Population of the British West India Colonies. Part I. Island of Jamaica. Taken before a Select Committee of the House of Lords, Session 1832. *London,* 1833

54—A Statement of the Objections of the Jamaica Proprietors resident in Great Britain to certain enactments in Mr. Secretary Stanley's Bill for the abolition of Slavery. *London,* 1833

55—Three Months in Jamaica in 1832 : Comprising a residence of seven weeks on a Sugar Plantation. By Henry Whiteley. *London,* 1833

The same. Verbatim Reprint. London, 1833

56—Claims for Compensation for Slaves, filed with the Assistant Commissioner for Jamaica. [No title.] 1835

57—Observations on the System by which Estates have been and are still managed in Jamaica; and on the apprenticeship introduced by the recent Abolition Act. By a Proprietor [Robert Paterson]. *Edinburgh,* 1836

58—A Statement of Facts illustrating the administration of the Abolition Law and the sufferings of the Negro apprentices in this island of Jamaica. *London,* 1837

59—A Statement of Facts submitted to the Right Hon. Lord Glenelg, His Majesty's Principal Secretary of State for the Colonies, Preparatory to an Appeal . . . to the Commons of Great Britain seeking redress for grievances . . . under the Administration of the Marquis of Sligo, the late Governor, and Sir Joshua Rowe, the present Lord Chief Justice of the Island of Jamaica, with an exposure of the present system of Jamaica Apprenticeship. By Henry Sterne. *London,* 1837

60—Memoir of a West Indian Planter [in Jamaica]. By the Rev. J. Riland. With an address to the Right Honourable Lord Glenelg on the present state of Colonial Slavery. *London,* 1837

61—A Narrative of Events since the first of August 1834. By James Williams, an apprenticed labourer in Jamaica. *London,* [1837]

The same. A Narrative of Events [in Jamaica] since the 1st of August 1834. Together with the evidence taken under a commission appointed by the Colonial Office to assertain the truth of the narrative; and the Report of the Commissioners thereon : the whole exhibiting a correct picture of a large proportion of West Indian Society, and the atrocious cruelties perpetrated under the Apprenticeship System. By James Williams, [with plate]. 8vo. *London,* 1838

62—Jamaica under the Apprenticeship System. By a Proprietor [Peter Howe, 2nd Marquess of Sligo]. *London,* 1838

63—The West Indies in 1837. Being the Journal of a visit to Antigua, Montserrat, Dominica, St. Lucia, Barbados and Jamaica. Undertaken for the purpose of ascertaining the actual condition of the negro population of those Islands. By Joseph Sturge and Thomas Harvey. *London,* 1838

The same. 2nd ed. *London,* 1838

64—Emancipation in the West Indies. A Six Months' Tour in Antigua, Barbados, and Jamaica in the year, 1837. By James A. Thome and J. Horace Kimball. *New York,* 1838

65—Jamaica Plantership. By Benjamin M'Mahon. *London,* 1839

66—Parliamentary Papers relative to the West Indies. 36 vols. folio ; 1835-47 :—

1835, Vol. I. Abolition of Slavery in the British Colonies (Jamaica, Barbadoes, British Guiana and Mauritius, 1833-35). Return of the several periods of Residence of the Bishops of Jamaica and Barbadoes within their respective Dioceses since their appointment.

1836, Vol. I. Abolition of Slavery in the British Colonies Jamaica (continued).

1836, Vol. IV. Abolition of Slavery in Jamaica. Negro Education. . . .

1837, Vol. I. Abolition of Slavery throughout the British Colonies. Jamaica. . . .

1838, Vol. I. Abolition of Slavery throughout the British Colonies. . . Copy of a Report from C. J. Latrobe, Esq., on Negro Education in Jamaica, with correspondence relating thereto

1839, Vol. I. Papers on the condition of the labouring population in the West Indies. Part I., Jamaica and British Guiana.

1839, Vol. IV. Papers on the condition of the labouring population in the West Indies, &e. . . Report of Hall Pringle and Alexander Campbell on the atrocities of slave traders,(Jamaica). Correspondence relative to the conduct of the negro population, Jamaica. Report of Capt. Milne of H.M.S. Snake, relative to certain atrocities alleged to have been perpetrated on board a Portuguese slaver, captured by the Snake, &c. Applications for bounties for capture of slave vessels. Copy of extracts from any further communication made to Her Majesty's Secretary of State, by the agent for Jamaica, relative. to the state of that island. An account of the value of all exports from Great Britain to Jamaica from the year 1830 to the present time; distinguishing each year. . . Papers relative to Jamaica. Copies of Acts passed by the Legislature of the island of Jamaica. Correspondence relating to the affairs of Jamaica. Copy of Memorial of the Association of Jamaica Proprietors. Copy of Memorial of Mr. Joseph Woodhead on behalf of the officers and crew of Her Majesty's brig Buzzard, as captors of the Spanish schooner Circe, illegally fitted for the traffic in slaves.

1839. Vol. V. Papers on the condition of the labouring population, West Indies, Part 1-5, Jamaica, continued . . Communications relative to the agricultural state of Jamaica.

1840, Vol. I. . . . Temporary Barracks at Maroon Town, Jamaica. Correspondence relating to the issue of fresh meat rations to the troops in Jamaica, the West Indies, and Bermuda.

1840, Vol. II. Papers relative to the affairs of Jamaica.

Papers relative to the Labouring Population of the British Colonies, and the general condition of the island of Jamaica, with copies of any memorials to Her Majesty from the island of Jamaica, respecting the Sugar Duties, together with copies of the replies thereto. *London*, 1845, 1847, 1849.

1844, Vol. II. Correspondence with the British Commissioners at Sierra Leone, Havanna, Rio de Janeiro, Surinam, the Cape of Good Hope, Jamaica, St. Paul de Loanda, and Boa Vista, relating to the Slave Trade, 1843.

1846, Vol. I. Correspondence with the British Commissioners at Sierra Leone. Havanna, Rio de Janeiro, Surinam, Cape of Good Hope, Jamaica, Loanda. amd Boa Vista, relating to the Slave Trade.

1847, Vol. I. Correspondence with the British Commissioners at Sierra Leone, Havanna, Rio de Janeiro, Surinam, Cape of Good Hope, Jamaica, Loanda, and Boa Vista, and Proceelings of British Vice-Admiralty Courts, relating to the Slave Trade, from January 1st to December 31st, 1846.

1847, Vol. II. Correspondence with the British Commissioners at Sierra Leone, Havanna, Rio de Janeiro, Surinam, Cape of Good Hope, Jamaica, Loanda, and Boa Vista.

1847. Returns showing the number of Free Emigrants into Jamaica, British Guiana, Trinidad and the Mauritius, since the abolition of Slavery in 1834; the number of Liberated Africans, and their destination, and the number of Emigrant Labourers now ordered by the above Colonies.

67—JAMAICA ENSLAVED AND FREE. [By Rev. B. Luckock]. *London*, [1846]

68—THE JAMAICA MOVEMENT for promoting the enforcement of the

Slave-Trade Treaties and the Suppression of the Slave Trade; with statement of Fact, Convention and Law. Prepared at the request of the Kingston Committee. [Edited by David Turnbull]. 4 vols. *London,* 1850

69—*STATEMENT OF FACTS relative to the island of Jamaica. *London,* 1852

70—THE UNCLE TOMS AND ST. CLARES OF JAMAICA. By a Stipendiary Magistrate [Stephen Bourne] in that island, during and subsequent to the apprenticeship. *London,* 1853

71—THE BRITISH WEST INDIA COLONIES in connection with Slavery, Emancipation, &c. By a Resident in the West Indies for thirteen years [Mrs. Campbell, née Bourne]. With an introduction and concluding remarks by a late Stipendiary Magistrate [Stephen Bourne]. 2nd ed. *London,* 1853

72—DEATH STRUGGLES OF SLAVERY. Being a narrative of facts and incidents, which occurred in a British Colony [Jamaica] during the two years immediately preceding negro emancipation. By [Rev.] Henry Bleby. *London,* 1853

*The same. 2nd ed.

The same. 3rd ed. *London,* 1868

73—THE NEGRO AND JAMAICA. By Commander Bedford Pim, R.N. Read before the Anthropological Society of London, Feb. 1st, 1866. *London,* 1866

74—JAMAICA, ITS STATE AND PROSPECTS; with an exposure of the Proceedings of the Freed-man's Aid Society, and the Baptist Missionary Society. *London,* 1867

II. IV. MAROONS.

75—PROCEEDING OF THE HONOURABLE HOUSE OF ASSEMBLY [Jamaica] relative to the Maroons; including the correspondence between the Right Honourable Earl Balcarres and the Honourable Major General Walpole, during the Maroon rebellion; with the Report of the joint Special Secret Committee, to whom those papers were referred. *St. Jago de la Vega,* 1796

76—THE PROCEEDINGS OF THE GOVERNOR AND ASSEMBLY OF JAMAICA, in regard to the Maroon Negroes: Published by order of the Assembly, to which is prefixed an introductory account [by Bryan Edwards], containing observations on the disposition, character, manners and habits of life, of the Maroons, and a detail of the origin, progress, and termination of the late war between those people and the white inhabitants. *London,* 1796

77—THE HISTORY OF THE MAROONS from their origin to the establishment of their chief Tribe at Sierra Leone; including the expedition to Cuba, for the purpose of procuring Spanish Chasseurs; and the state of the island of Jamaica for the last ten years: with a succinct History of the island previous to that period. By R[obert] C[harles] Dallas. [Illustrated]. 2 vols. *London,* 1803

The same. Geschichte der Maronen-Negern auf Jamaika, nebst einer Schilderung des vermaligen und jetzigen Zustandes dieser Insel. Aus dem Englischen, herausgegeben von T. F. Ehrmann. *Weimar,* 1805

II. V. DISTURBANCES.

78—*NARRATIVE OF CERTAIN EVENTS connected with the late Disturbances in Jamaica, and the charges preferred against the Baptist Missionaries in that island. Published by order of the Committee of the [Baptist Missionary] Society. *London,* 1832

79—DEFENCE OF THE BAPTIST MISSIONARIES from the charge of inciting the late Rebellion in Jamaica, in a discussion between the Rev. William Knibb and Mr. P. Barthwick at the Assembly Rooms, Bath on December 15th 1832 . * * *London* 1832

80—FACTS AND DOCUMENTS connected with the late insurrection in Jamaica, and the Violations of Civil and Religious Liberty arising out of it. [By Rev. William Knibb?] *London,* 1832

81—JAMAICA PAPERS, No. 1. Facts

and Documents relating to the alleged Rebellion in Jamaica, and the Measures of repression; including notes of the trial of Mr. Gordon. Published by the Jamaica Committee. *London*, 1866

82—JAMAICA PAPERS No. II. The Blue Books. Published by the Jamaica Committee. *London*, n. d. [?1866].

82a—*JAMAICA PAPERS, No. III.

83b—*JAMAICA PAPERS, No. IV.

83—JAMAICA PAPERS No. V. Martial Law. Six Letters to "The Daily News." By Frederic Harrison. Published by the Jamaica Committee. *London*, 1867

84—JAMAICA PAPERS No. VI. Illustrations of Martial Law in Jamaica. Compiled from the report of the Royal Commissioners, and other Blue Books laid before Parliament. By John Gorrie. Published by the Jamaica Committee. *London*, 1867

85—JAMAICA PAPERS No. VII. Report of the Proceedings at Bow Street Police Station on the Committal of Colonel Nelson and Lieutenant Brand for the murder of Mr. G. W. Gordon. Edited from the shorthand writer's notes by William Shaen, M. A. Published by the Jamaica Committee. *London*, 1867

86—PARLIAMENTARY PAPERS. Vol. I. Papers relative to the affairs of Jamaica. Presented to Parliament Feb. 1866. Vol. II. Papers relating to the Disturbances in Jamaica; Pts. I, II. and III. Feb. 1866. Reports of the Jamaica Royal Commission, 1866, Pt. I., Report. Copy of a despatch from the Right Hon. Edward Cardwell, M.P., to Lieut.-Genl. Sir H. K. Storks, G.C.B., G.C.M.G . Governor in-chief of the Island of Jamaica. Vol. III. Report of the Jamaica Royal Commission, 1866. Pt. II. Minutes of evidence and appendix. Vol. IV. Jamaica Disturbances, Papers laid before the Royal Commission of Inquiry by Governor Eyre. 4 vols. *London*, 1866

87—THE REIGN OF TERROR. A narrative of facts concerning Ex-Governor Eyre, George William Gordon, and the Jamaica Atrocities. By [Rev.] Henry Bleby. *London*, 1868

88—THE CASE OF GEORGE WILLIAM GORDON: with Preliminary Observations on the Jamaica Riot of Oct. 11, 1865. By Baptist Wriottesley Noel. *London*, 1866

89—* A NARRATIVE OF THE REBELLIOUS OUTBREAK in Jamaica, October 11, 1865. An account of the massacre and my own providential escape. By Arthur Warmington, J. P. and Lieutenant of Volunteers (unattached), Jamaica. *Tottenham, London,* [1866]

90—JAMAICA AND THE COLONIAL OFFICE, Who caused the crisis ? By George Price. *London*, 1866

91—CHARGE OF THE LORD CHIEF JUSTICE of England to the Grand Jury . . in the case of the Queen against Nelson and Brand . . Revised and corrected by the Lord Chief Justice, Sir Alexander Cockburn, Bart. Edited by Frederick Cockburn, *London*, 1867

92—THE HISTORY OF THE JAMAICA CASE, being an account founded upon official documents of the Rebellion of the Negroes in Jamaica. By W. F. Finlason, 2nd ed., enlarged and corrected. *London*, 1869.

93—THE TRAGEDY OF MORANT BAY. A Narrative of the Disturbances in the island of Jamaica in 1865. By Edward Bean Underhill, LL.D. *London*, 1895

II. VI.   NAVAL MILITARY AND CONSTABULARY.

94—A TRUE ACCOUNT OF THE TRYALS AND ARRAIGNMENTS OF COL. RICHARD KIRKBY, Capt. John Constable, Capt. Cooper Wade, Capt. Samuel Vincent and Capt. Christopher Fogg, on a complaint exhibited by the Judge-Advocate on behalf of Her Majesty, at a Court-Martial held on board the ship Bredah, in Port Royal Harbour, in Jamaica, in America, the 8th, 9th, 10th, and 12th days of October, 1702; for Cowardice, Newlect (*sic*) of Duty, Breach of Orders and other Crimes, committed by them in a fight at sea, commenced the 19th of August, 1702, off St. Martha, in the latitude of ten degrees north, near the Mainland of America between the Honourable John

Benbow, Esq., and Admiral Du Casse with four French ships of war. For which Colonel Kirkby and Captain Wade were sentenced to be shot to death. Transmitted from two eminent merchants at Port Royal, in Jamaica, to a person of quality in the City of London. *London,* 1703

95—AN ACCOUNT OF THE TRIAL OF FRANCIS DELAP, Esq., late Provost-Marshal-General, upon an information for a misdemeanor : at a Supreme Court of Judicature, held in the town of Kingston in the island of Jamaica on June 18th, 1755. *London,* 1755

96—*MINUTES OF A COURT MARTIAL at Port Royal on Captain Roddam of H. M. S. " Greenwich," *Kingston,* 1757

97—* A BRIEF HISTORY of the late Expition against Fort San Juan, so far as it relates to the diseases of the troops ; together with some observations on climate, infection and contagion. By Thomas Dancer. *Kingston,* 1781

98—* SYSTEM OF EXERCISE and Manœuvres for the Kingston Regiment of Foot Militia. *Kingston,* 1792

99—LOSS OF HIS MAJESTY'S SHIP CENTAUR, of seventy-four guns, the 23d of September, 1782 ; and miraculous preservation of the Pinnace with the Captain, Master, and ten of the crew, also the Explosion of the French East-India Company's vessel the Prince, on the 25th of July 1752 and miraculous preservation of part of the crew in the Pinnace. *London.* n. d.

100—PROCEEDINGS OF A GENERAL COURT-MARTIAL held [on Major Allan Cameron] in Kingston Barracks in the island of Jamaica, March 10, 1802, by order of His Excellency Major-General George Nugent. *London,* 1802

101—* THE FIRST REPORT of the Commissioners of Naval Enquiry, appointed by Act 43, Geo III. Naval Storekeepers at Jamaica. 1803

102—PROCEEDINGS OF THE GENERAL COURT MARTIAL assembled by order of His Excellency General Nugent, Lieut-Governor . . . of Jamaica, for the Trial of David Murray, Esq., a Commissioner appointed for the parish of Westmoreland, for procuring subsistence for the Militia and for other duties. Held in Spanish Town the 8th and 9th July 1805 . . . . . *Kingston,* 1805

103—INSTRUCTIONS FOR THE DRILL, Formation and Movements of the Militia of Jamaica : by authority. *Jamaica,* 1827

104—RETURNS made under the Militia Law (1840). *Jamaica.* mss.

105—* RULES AND REGULATIONS for the Jamaica Constabulary Force, approved and confirmed by . . . Sir J. P. Grant, Governor-in Chief. *Spanish Town,* 1867

106—RULES AND REGULATIONS for the guidance and general government of the Jamaica Constabulary Force . . . together with an epitome of the Laws applicable to the Constabulary. Compiled and arranged by A[ugustus] C[onstantine] Sinclair, under the direction of Captain K. H. A. Mainwaring, R. N. *Kingston,* 1876

107—THE HISTORY OF THE FIRST WEST INDIA REGIMENT. By Major A[lfred] B[urdon] Ellis. (Coloured plates and maps). *London,* 1885

108—NEW EDITION of the Firing Exercise Snider-Enfield Rifle and Carbine. Revised for the use of the Jamaica Volunteer Militia. *Kingston,* 1887

109—KINGSTON SAILORS HOME—Ninth, twelfth and fourteenth to twenty-first Annual Meetings. *Kingston,* 1888-1901

110—THE JAMAICA CONSTABULARY LIST and Directory, 1897. Compiled with the approval of the Inspector-General of Police. By Harry McCrea. *Kingston,* 1897

111—ONE HUNDRED YEAR'S HISTORY OF THE 2nd BATT. WEST INDIA REGIMENT from date of raising 1795 to 1898. By Col. J[ames] E.[W.S.] Caulfield. [With illustrations]. *London,* 1899

112—THE CAPTURE OF SANTIAGO, in Cuba, by Captain Myngs, 1662. By C. H. Firth. (Re-printed from the English Historical Review). 1899

II. VII. CHURCH HISTORY.

113—RELIGIOUS PERSECUTION IN JA-
MAICA. Report of the Speeches of
the Rev. Peter Duncan, Wesleyan
Missionary and the Rev. W. Knibb,
Baptist Missionary . . August
15, 1832. 3rd ed. *London,*   1832

114—A NARRATIVE OF RECENT EVENTS
connected with the Baptist Mission
in this island [Jamaica], comprising
also a sketch of the Mission from
its commencement in 1814, to the
end of 1831. By the Baptist Missionaries. *Kingston,*   1833

115—BRIEF NOTICE of the Rise, Progress and present State of the Jamaica Clergy Fund.   [1834]

116—*ON CONVERSION. The first circular letter of the Baptist Missionaries
to the Churches in Jamaica. *Jamaica,*   1836

117—A CALL TO HIS PARISHIONERS. By
George Wilson Bridges, Rector of
St. Ann, Jamaica. *Falmouth, 1837*

118—AN ANSWER TO THE OBJECTIONS of
the Rev. Thomas Pennock against
" Methodism as it is" as published
in the Jamaica Watchman. By
David Kerr. *Montego Bay,*   1838

119—THE CHURCH CONSTITUTION of the
Jamaica Wesleyan Association.
Kingston,   1839

120—REV. WILLIAM KNIBB'S SPEECH.
Proceedings of the Public Meeting
held in Exeter Hall, May 22, 1840,
on occasion of the public reception
of the Rev. Wm. Knibb, H. Beckford, and E. Barrett. *London,* 1840

121—FIVE VIEWS OF BAPTIST CHÁPELS
in Jamaica. *London,*   1840

122—A GENTILE'S ENTREATY: Addresses to the Jews in Jamaica. By
J. J. Freeman. *London,*   [1843]

123—A CHARGE DELIVERED at the Primary Visitation of the Clergy of
the Archdeaconry of Jamaica in
the cathedral-church of St. Jago
de la Vega, 12th Dec., 1844, by
Aubrey George [Spencer] Lord
Bishop of Jamaica. *Spanish Town,*
  1845

124—REPORTS OF THE JAMAICA DIOCE-
SAN CHURCH SOCIETY for 1846, 1847,
1850. *Kingston.*   1846-50

125—THE WELEYAN METHODIST MIS-
SION IN JAMAICA and Honduras deli-
neated, containing a description of
the principal stations. Together
with a conservative account of the
Rise and Progress of Work of the
God at each. Illustrated . . .
By the Rev. Peter Samuel, twelve
years a Missionary in Jamaica.
London,   1850
The same. Aberdeen,   1850

126—A NARRATIVE OF THE WESLEYAN
MISSION TO JAMAICA; with occasional remarks on the State of Society in that Colony. By the Rev
Peter Duncan. *London,*   1849

127—RULES OF THE CHURCH SOCIETY
for the propagation of the Gospel
in the Archdeaconry of Middlesex
in Jamaica. *Spanish Town,* 1853

128—REPORT OF THE CHURCH SOCIETY
for the propagation of the Gospel in
the Archdeaconry of Middlesex in
Jamaica. *Spanish Town,*   1854

129—THE MORAVIANS IN JAMAICA.
History of the Mission of the United
Brethren's Church to the Negroes
in the island of Jamaica, from the
year 1754 to 1854. By J. H. Buchner. *London,*   1854

130—THE SURREY CHURCH SOCIETY for
the propagation of the Gospel and
the promotion of Religious Education. Report for 1854. *Spanish
Town,*   1855

131—*A LETTER FROM JAMAICA [on the
subject of religious revivals. By
W. W. T.]. *London,*   [1860]

132—REPORTS OF THE JAMAICA CHURCH
OF ENGLAND Home and Foreign
Missionary Society for the years
1862 to 1900. *Kingston,* 1862-1901
[Missing from set in Institute, 6th
8th, 9th, 13th, 29th, and 37th].

133—TWENTY-NINE YEARS IN THE WEST
INDIES and Central Africa: a review of missionary work and ad-
venture 1829-1858. By the Rev.
Hope Masterton Waddell. *London,*   1863

134—THE VOICE OF JUBILEE. A Narrative of the Baptist Mission, Jamaica, from its commencement;
with biographical notices of its
fathers and founders. By John
Clark, W. Dendy and J. M. Phil-

lippo. With an introduction by David J. East. *London,* 1865

135—CHRISTIAN DUTIES VIEWED AS Social, Religious and Civil : illustrated and enforced. By the Rev. James Watson. *Kingston,* 1866

136—MEMORIALS OF BAPTIST MISSIONARIES in Jamaica, including a sketch of the labours of early religious instructors in Jamaica. By John Clarke. *London,* 1869

137—SUGGESTIONS for the better selecting, preparing, and appointing the Catechists of the Church of England in Jamaica, with remarks on honorary lay-readers. [By Rev. D. H. Campbell and Rev. E. Nuttall]. *Kingston,* 1869

138—JOURNALS of the 1st to 33rd Annual Synods, and three Special Synods, of the Church of England in Jamaica. *Kingston,* 1869-1902

139—RESOLUTIONS of Diocesan Council, Correspondence, and opinion of Attorney-General, relating to the jurisdiction of the Synod of the Church of England in Jamaica. *Kingston,* 1871

140—MEMORIAL OF THE DIOCESAN COUNCIL of the Church of England in Jamaica to the British Government, in reference to the claims of of the Bishop of Kingston for the continuance of his stipend from the consolidated fund : with a preparatory statement. *London,* 1872

141—RISE AND PROGRESS OF WESLEYAN-METHODISM in Jamaica. By [Rev.] Henry Blaine Foster. *London,* 1881

142—NABOTH'S VINEYARD or the Law and Justice of the Wesleyan Methodist New Departure in Jamaica. *Kingston,* 1885

143—HOME LIFE IN JAMAICA. A Letter respectfully addressed to Ministers of Religion, January 1st 1885. [By H.]. *Kingston,* 1885

144—THE CALENDAR of the Jamaica Church Theological College. Advent, 1886 : to which are appended regulations respecting candidates for ordination in the Diocese of Jamaica. *Kingston,* 1886

145—DIOCESE OF JAMAICA. PAROCHIAL MISSION, 1887. Address by the Bishop [E. Nuttall] to Clergy and Lay-helpers delivered at a Conference held in Spanish Town, August 12th, 1887. *Kingston,* 1887

146—ST. ANDREW'S PARISH CHURCH Rectory, Missions and School-rooms. *Jamaica,* 1888

147—A SHORT SKETCH of the History of the Church of England in Jamaica. By Rev. J[ohn] B. Ellis, M. A., *Kingston,* 1891

148—A PLEA FOR THE AGNOSTIC. By A. M. Mould. *Kingston,* 1892

149—REPORTS OF THE KINGSTON PARISH CHURCH for 1891, 1895. *Kingston,* 1892 and 1895

150—THE STORY OF OUR JAMAICA MISSION with sketch of our Trinidad Mission. By George Robson, D.D. (Mission of the United Presbyterian Church). *Edinburgh,* 1894

151—THE CHURCHMAN'S MANUAL. A Book of Instruction and Devotion intended chiefly of the use of Members of the Church of England in Jamaica. By the Most Rev. Enos Nuttall, D.D. *Kingston,* 1893
The same. London and New York, 1894

152—ADDRESS delivered by the Most Rev. the Lord Bishop of Jamaica, on 30th January, 1894, during the opening sitting of the Synod of the Church of England in Jamaica. *Kingston,* [1894]

153—THE CONGREGATION OF UNITED BRETHREN or Moravians at Fairfield, Jamaica. Reports and Statistics. *Kingston,* 1895

154—THE CHRISTIAN HOME LIFE. A paper prepared by the Rev. S. J. Washington for discussion at the Ministerial Conference of the Jamaica Baptist Union held . . Feb., 1895. *Kingston,* 1895

155—JAMAICA CHRISTIAN ENDEAVOUR UNION. Reports of the Annual Conventions held in Kingston in 1894, 1895, 1896, 1897, 1898, 1899, 1900, 1901. *Kingston,* 1895-1901

156—PAROCHIAL COUNCIL FOR THE PARISH OF TRELAWNY. Report for 1895. *Kingston,* 1896

157—ARE CATHOLICS IDOLATORS ? Full Account of the Controversy between Bishop Gordon and Bishop Nuttall. *Kingston,* 1896

158—The Worship of the Virgin Mary and other points of Controversy. By the Bishop of Jamaica, [Enos Nuttall, D. D.] in reply to the Bishop of Thyatira [C. Gordon, S.J.]. *Kingston,*   1896

159—Some Present Needs of Jamaica as specified in an address at the opening meeting of the Diocesan Synod on 9th February, 1897. By the Most Rev. the Lord Bishop of Jamaica, Primate of the West Indies [Enos Nuttall]. *Kingston,* 1897

160—Parochial Council for the Parish of Hanover. Report for 1896. *Kingston,*   897

161—Constitutions and Canons of the Church of England in Jamaica. Re-printed by authority of the Diocesan Synod, 1897. With Appendix. *Kingston,*   1897

Bound with the above :—

Amendments to the Canons, made from 1897 to 1901.

162—St. Michael's Church, Kew Park Westmoreland, Jamaica. Consecrated by the Archbishop of the West Indies, 7th December.   1893

163—Statement and Appeal by the Archbishop of the West Indies (Enos Nuttall) respecting Church and Educational Work and Needs in the Diocese of Jamaica. [*Kingston*], 1898

164—St. Andrew's Presbyterian Church [Kingston] Jubilee Souvenir, 1848-1898. *Kingston* [1898]

165—A Book of Special Services together with special prayers. Authorized for use in the Diocese of Jamaica. By the Most Rev Enos Nuttall, D.D. 2nd ed. revised and enlarged. *London,*   1900

166—The Archbishop's [Enos Nuttall] Address to the Diocesan Synod of Jamaica, February 5th, 1901

167—Report of the Parish Church of the Parish of St. Andrew for the year 1900. *Kingston,*   1901

168—Report of the Catholic Union and Sodality, for the year 1900. *Kingston,*   1901

II. viii. Topography.

Bath.

169—A Short Dissertation on the Jamaica Bath Waters, to which is prefixed an introduction concerning Mineral Waters in general : shewing the Methods of examining them and ascertaining their Contents. By Thomas Dancer, M. D. *Kingston,*   1784
[Bound with the above]—
Some observations respecting the Botanical Garden. *Jamaica,* 1804

Kingston.

170—Account current 1809-1819; 1819-1834; 1846-49; 1851-57. (ms.)

171—Almoner's Roll, 1872. (ms.)

172—Assessment Book, 1842-49 and West Division, 1848. 3 vols. (ms) Assessment Roll, 1841, 1846, 1846-57. 3 vols. (ms.)

173—Capitation Tax Roll, 1843. (ms.)

174—The Cause of Resignation of his office explained, with a vindication of his conduct. By James Scott, M.R.C.S. Eng., late Commissioner of Health for Kingston. *Kingston,*   1884

175—Church-wardens' Accounts, 1722-1759, 1771-1786, 1835-1848.

176—City Accounts, 1820-1844. (ms.)

177—City Bonds, 1786-1830. (ms.)

178—Claims to Vote, 1835-1837, 1838-1841, 1841-1858. 2 vols. (ms.)

179—Common Council, Proceedings of : 1795-1803 ; 1803-1815 ; 1815-1820 ; 1820-28; 1850-54 ; 1862-66. 6 vols. (ms.)

180—Minutes : 1828-1839 , 1845-1858 ; 1862-1866. (ms.)
Rough Minute Book, 1819-21 ; 1843-44 ; 1846-48. 3 vols. (ms.)
Special Committee Minute Book, 1842-50. (ms.)

181—Account Current, 1851-54. (ms.)

182—Copies of Deeds, 1806-1840. (ms.)

183—Letter Book, 1863-67. (ms.)

184—Pleas Judgment, 1819-1825. (ms.)

185—Directory, 1878. [Containing a General Business and Street Directory of Kingston   . Spanish Town . . . the entire island and a special Directory

of Estates and Properties
Compiled by R. H. Ives. *Ja-maica,* 1878

186—Hospital Accounts, 1804-1818 : 1819-34 ; 1835. (ms.)

187—List of Taxpayers, East Division, 1852. (ms.)

188—Militia Register. (ms.)

189—Out Pensioners Book, 1853-1866, 1867. (ms.)

190—Papers relating to the present sanitary state of Kingston, Jamaica. Printed for circulation. *Kingston,* 1874.

191—Parish Tax,1750-54 ; 1754 ; 1763-67 ; 1768-70 ; 1774-80 ; 1880-1805 ; 1837-43. 7 vols. (ms.)

192—Poll Tax, 1792-1805 and 1819-1835. 2 vols. (ms.)

193—Quarter Sessions, Proceedings of the, 1770-1798 and 1803-39. 2 vols. (ms.)

194—Quit Rent Roll, 1835-41. (ms.)

195—Record of persons who have paid their taxes. East Division 1859-57. (ms.)

196—Register of Births, 1844-1853. (ms.)

197—Register of Deaths, 1844-54. (ms.)

198—Register of Freeholders, 1803-1832. (ms.)

199—Register of Slaves, 1761 95. (ms.)

200—Register of Porters and Carriers, 1840. (ms.)

201—Register of Voters, 1864-66. (ms.)

202—Regulations for the City and parish of Kingston including the May Pen Cemetery Rules. . . also Hackney Carriage Regulations, Boat Regulations, Fire Brigade Rules, By-Laws of the Local Board of Health and the Kingston Theatre. *Kingston,* 1898

203—Relief Assessment Book, West Division, 1851. (ms) Relief Roll, 1850. East Division, 1847-50. West Division, 1848. 2 vols. (ms)

204—Reports of the Commissioner of Health, Kingston, Jamaica, for 1874, 1875, 1876, 1877, 1878, 1879, 1881, 1882, 1883, 1884 *Kingston.*

205—Reports of the Engineer of the Kingston and Liguanea Water Works for the year 1878, 1879, 1880, By-Laws and Scales of Rates 1882 Reports for 1883, 1884, 1885, 1887, *Kingston.*

206—Reports of the Engineer of the Kingston Gas Works for the years 1879, 1880, 1881, 1882, 1883, 1884, 1885, 1886, 1887. *Kingston.*

207—Report of the City Surveyor 1891. *Kingston,* 1892

208—Report on the Proposed Sewerage of Kingston. By Osbert Chadwick, C.E., C.M.G. *Kingston,* 1893

209—Retailers of Sprit, 1825-27, and persons recommended for public relief, 1835-38. (ms.)

210—Return of Coroners Inquests held in the city and parish of Kingston . . April 1846—March 1847. By Benjamin Naar. *Kingston,* 1847

211—Return of Taxable Property, 1862 West Division ; 1863 East Division, and 1866-67. 3 vols. (ms.)

212—Return Roll : Real and Personal Property, East Division, 1857. (ms) Rough Roll Public and Parish Tax, East Division, 1845-46, 1850, 1853-57. West Division, 1840-53, 1842. 5 vols. (ms.)

213—St. Michael's Chapel Committee, 1842-65. (ms.)

214—Taxpayers, Alphabetical List of : East Division, 1843, 1844-5, 1849-52. West Division, 1844, 1848 and 1850. 5 vols. (ms.)

215—Supplemental Tax and Surcharge Roll. West Division, 1849. (ms.)

216—Tax Roll, 1853 ; East Division, 1842, 1844, 1852, 1854 : West Division, 1848, 1850, 1851. West Division, 1851, 1855, and 1857. (ms.)

217—Tax Relief Roll, 1843-49, 1844-45. East Division, 1846 : West Division, 1849. 4 vols. (ms.)

218—Titles of Lands, 1833-41. (ms.)

219—Toll Book : Slaves Sold, 1738-43. (ms.)

220—Vestry Minutes, 1744-49, 1781-88. 2 vols. (ms.)

221—Vestry Accounts, 1760-92. (ms.)

222—Weekly Allowance Record. (ms.)

MANCHESTER—

323—Statistical History of the parish of Manchester, in the island of Jamaica. By the Rev. George W[ilson] Bridges. *Jamaica, 1824*

PORT ROYAL—

324—Accounts, 1842-1852 (m).

325—Church Tax. (ms.)

326—Church Wardens Accounts, 1766-1793 and 1818–1830. (ms).

327—Claims to vote, 1835-1857. (ms.)

328—Convictions, 1834-1837. (ms.)

329—Freehold Book, 1756-1803. (ms.)

230—Receipt Book, 1807-1826, 1826-1834. 5 vols. (ms.)

231—Register of Title of Land, 1805-1841. (ms.)

232—Relief Roll, 1852-1857 (ms.)

233—Return of Slaves, 1817, 1820, 1826. (ms.)

234—Sale of Slaves, 1783-1794, 1800-1806. (ms.)

235—Summary Slave Trials, 1819-34.

236—Tax Roll, 1841-47, 1849-57. (ms.)

237—Vestry Minutes, 1735-1741, 1788-1807, 1819-1866. (ms.)

238—A WEEK AT PORT ROYAL [By Richard Hill]. *Montego Bay,* 1855

239—PORT ROYAL AND ITS HARBOUR. With short notes on its History, Legends, Sports, Pastimes and Avocations. By Major M. M[artin] and others. *Jamaica,* 1893

ST. CATHERINE—

240— MONUMENTS OF THE CATHEDRAL-CHURCH and Parish of St. Catharine: being Pt. I. of Church Notes and Monumental Inscriptions of Jamaica, in the year 1824. By John Roby. *Montego Bay,* 1831

ST. JAMES—

241—THE HISTORY OF THE PARISH OF ST. JAMES, in Jamaica, with notes on the General History, Genealogy and Monumental Inscriptions of the island. By John Roby. Part I. [with ms. notes by the author]. *Jamaica,* 1848

The same. Kingston, 1849

ST. MARY—

242—THE HANDBOOK OF THE PARISH OF ST. MARY. By Ralph M. Cocking. . . . *Kingston,* 1894

The same for 1899. *Kingston, 1898*

SPANISH TOWN—

243—Report of a Committee of the House of Assembly of Jamaica respecting the Spanish Town and Porus Tramway. Correspondence between Lieutenant Governor Eyre and the Secretary of State since June 1862, respecting the Tramway. Extract from Lieutenant-Governor Eyre's speech in the Assembly on the 4th Nov. 1862, respecting the Spanish Town and Porus Tramway. Correspondence relating to Mr. Espeut.

244—THE GHOST AT JOHN CROW HOUSE. A Tale of Spanish Town (60 years ago). By W. Duncan Byles. *Kingston,* 1889

245—A FORTY-FIVE YEARS REMINISCENCE of the Characteristics and Characters of Spanish Town. A lecture delivered . . 31st July, 1890 . by W. A. Feurtado. *Kingston,* 1890

246—HOTEL RIO COBRE, Spanish Town, Jamaica, 1893. *Kingston,* 1893

247—OLD SAINT JAGO. By G. F. J[udah]. *Kingston,* 1896

—

248—JAMAICA CARTOGRAPHY. Chronological List of the Maps of Jamaica in the Library of the Institute of Jamaica, both on separate sheets and in books: with some notes on the history of the parishes of the island. By Frank Cundall, F.S.A. (Reprinted from "The Handbook of Jamaica for 1897"). *Kingston,* 1897

II. ix. MISCELLANEOUS EPISODES IN JAMAICA HISTORY.

249—*A SAD AND TERRIBLE RELATION of the dreadful Earthquake that happened at Jamaica, 7 June 1692; also an account of the utter defeat of the French then landed there. *London,* 1692

250—THE TRUEST AND LARGEST ACCOUNT of the late Earthquake in Jamaica, June 7th, 1692. Written by a Reverend Divine there [of Withywood in Vere] to his friend in London. With some improvements thereof by another hand [H. L]. *London,* 1693

251—*An Account of the Earthquake of 1692 at Port Royal. By the Rector [E. Heath]. 1692

252—Practical Reflections on the late Earthquake in Jamaica, . . . Anno 1692. . . . Lon on, 1693

253— Three Physico-Theological Discourses . . . wherein are largely discussed . . . the Nature and Causes of Earthquakes; with an Historical Account of those two late Remarkable ones in Jamaica and England. London, 1693

254—A True Account of the late Pyracies of Jamaica : the authors, abettors and encouragers thereof. With other transactions relating thereto. By one just arrived from that island. To which is added a genuine letter to a very Eminent Personage concerned [Dr. Samuel Page]. 2nd. ed. with large notes explaining the whole to the satisfaction of the Reader. London, 1716

255—A Genuine Account of Earthquakes, especially that at Oxford in the year 1683 and of another terrible one at Port Royal, in Jamaica, in 1692. London, 1750

256—The Theory and History of Earthquakes : containing . . a particular and authentic history of those which have happened in . . Jamaica . . . London, n.d.

257—History of Jamaica and Barbados. With an authentic account of the lives lost and the damages sustained in each island by the late hurricanes . . 1781

258—The Brig Nancy. In the Vice-Admiralty Court of Jamaica. The Advocate General in rel ; Wylie et al. Commander vs. The Brig Nancy, her guns, tackle, &c. Proceeding in Suit ; for Salvage ; filed in Court 9th September 1799, cause heard and vessel and cargo condemned on Monday, 25th November, 1799 . . . C. W. Alder, Proctor. (ms.)

259—Interesting Tracts relating to the Island of Jamaica, consisting of curious State-papers, Councils of war, Letters, Petitions, Narratives, &c., &c., which throw great light on the history of that island, from its conquest, down to the year 1702. St. Jago de la Vega, 1800.

260—Report of a Committee of the Honourable House of Assembly on the . . . Post Office Department [of Jamaica]. Jamaica, 1815

261—*Legend of Rose Hall Estate in the parish of St. James, Jamaica. Falmouth, 1823

262 The Picaroons, or one hundred and fifty years ago. Being a history of commerce and navigation in the West Indian Seas. By Richard Hill. (Communicated to the Port Royal Reading Society). Dublin, 1869

263—Papers connected with the Jubilee 1887 and Diamond Jubilee, 1897, Kingston, 1887 & 1897

264—Studies in Jamaica History. By Frank Cundall, F.S.A. With illustrations by Mrs. Lionel Lee. London, 1900

III. Descriptive Accounts.

265—*A True Description of Jamaica, with the fertility, commodities and healthfulness of the place. As also the towns, havens, creeks, promontories, and the circuit of the whole island. London, 1657

266—*Jamaica viewed with all the ports, harbours, and their several soundings, towns, and settlements thereunto belonging, together with the nature of its climate, fruitfulness of the soile, and its suitablenesse to English complexions. With several other collateral observations and reflexions upon the island. By E[dmund] H[ickeringill]. [With map]. London, 1661

The same. 2nd ed. London, 1661

The same. 3rd ed. [with portrait and new map]. London, 1705

267—A Description of the Island of Jamaica and other isles and territories in America, to which the English are related . . . Taken from the Notes of Sir Thomas Linch, Knight, Governor of Jamaica, and other experienced persons in the said places. Illustrated with maps. By Richard Blome. London, 1672

—The same. Recueil de Divers Voyages faits en Afrique et en l'Amerique, qui n'ont point esté encore publiez; contenant l'Origine, les Moeurs, les Coûtumes et le Commerce des habitans de ces deux Parties du Monde. . . . . (VI.) Description de l'isle de la Jamaique, et de toutes celles que possedent les Anglois dans l'Amerique. Avec des observations faites par le sieur Thomas [Lynch] gouverneur de la Jamaique, et autres personnes du Païs. *Paris,* 1674

The same. Together with the present state of Algiers. *London,* 1678

The same. The Present State of His Majesties Isles and Territories in America : viz : Jamaica . . . with new maps of every place . . . *London,* 1687

268—THE PRESENT STATE OF JAMAICA with the Life of the Great Columbus, the first Discoverer ; to which is added an exact accouut of Sir Henry Morgan's voyage to, and famous siege and taking of Panama from the Spaniards. *London,* 1683

269—A TRIP TO JAMAICA : with a true character of the People and Island. By the author of A Sot's Paradise [Edward Ward ("Ned Ward")]. 2nd ed. *London,* 1698

270—A VOYAGE TO THE ISLANDS Madera, Barbados, Nieves. S. Christopher's and Jamaica. With the Natural History of the Herbs and Trees, four-footed Beasts, Fishes, Birds, Insects, Reptiles, &c., of the last of those islands ; to which is prefixed an introduction wherein is an account of the Inhabitants, Air, Water, Diseases, Trade, &c. of that place, with some relations concerning the neighbouring Continent and islands of America. Illustrated with the figures of the things described, which have not been heretofore engraved. By [Sir] Hans Sloane [Bart]. 2 vols. *London,* 1707 and 1725

271—USEFUL TRANSACTIONS for the months of May, June, July, August and September, 1709. Containing a voyage to the Island of Cajamai in America. Giving a brief account of the natural Rarieties, Inhabitants and Diseases of the country;

together with their cures after the method used by Jasper Van Slonenbergh, a learned Member of the Royal Vertuosi of Great Britain in the relation he has given of his voyages into those parts. Translated into English from the Dutch. By Dr. William King, D.C.L. *London,* n.d.

272—THE STATE OF THE ISLAND of chiefly in relation to its Commerce and the conduct of the Spaniards in the West Indies. Addressed to a Member of Parliament by a person who resided several years at Jamaica [A...B...]. *London,* 1726

273—THE IMPORTANCE OF JAMAICA to Great Britain considered. With some account of that Island, from its discovery in 1492 [sic] to this Time, and a list of the Governors and Presidents, with an account of their towns, harbours, bays, buildings, inhabitants, whites and negroes, &c. . . . An account of their Fruits, Drugs, Timbers and Dying-woods and of the uses they are apply'd to here. . . . With an account of their Trade and Produce . . . . In a letter to a Gentleman. . . . . . *London,* [1740]

274—A LETTER FROM A FRIEND AT J—— [Dr. James Smith] to a Friend in London : giving an impartial account of the violent proceedings of the Faction in that Island. *London,* [1746]

275—* RELAZIONE DE . . terrimoti accaduti . . nell ' Isola de S. Domingo, della Giammaica, &c., 1752

276—LETTRE DE MR. . . . à Mr. S. B., Docteur en Médicine à Kingston, dans la Jamaïque, au sujét des Troubles qui agitent actuellement toute l'Amerique septentrionale. *La Haye,* 1776

277—REPONSE DE MR. J. DE PINTO, aux Observations d'un Homme impartial, sur sa Lettre à Mr. S. B., Docteur en médecine à Kingston, dans la Jamaïque au sujét des Troubles qui agitent actuellement toute l' Amérique septentrionale. *La Haye,* 1776

278—DESCRIPTION DE L'ISLE DE LA JA-
MAIQUE, Traduite de l'Anglois [an
article in the Universal Magazine
for 1773] par [Jean Claude] Pin-
geron. *Avignon,* 1782

279—CONSIDERATIONS UPON THE PROBA-
BILITY OF AN ATTACK on the island
of Jamaica. *London,* 1782

28 —AN ACCOUNT OF THE ISLAND OF
JAMAICA with Reflections on the
Treatment, Occupation and Provisions of the Slaves. To which is
added a Description of the Animal
and Vegetable Productions of the
Island. By a gentleman lately re
sident on a Plantation [Peter
Marsden]. *Newcastle,* 1788

281—A DESCRIPTIVE ACCOUNT OF THE
ISLAND OF JAMAICA. With remarks
upon the cultivation of the sugar
cane throughout the different seasons of the year, and chiefly considered in a picturesque point of
view. Also observations and reflections upon what would probably
be the consequences of an abolition
of the slave-trade, and of the emancipation of the slaves. By William
Beckford [of Somerly]. 2 vols. *London,* 1790

The same. VUES PITTORESQUES DE
LA JAMAIQUE, avec une Description
detaillée de ses productions, surtout
des cannes à sucre, des travaux, du
traitement et des moeurs des Nègres,
&c. Traduit de l'Anglais de M. W.
Beckfort (*sic*) par J. S. P. nouvelle
édition. 2 vols. *Lausanne,* 1793

282—ACCOUNT OF THE ISLAND AND GO-
VERNMENT OF JAMAICA written [by
Francis Hanson] in the year 1682,
and prefixed to the first printed
collection of the laws; *Contains also*
(*i*) A Proclamation for the encouraging of Planters in His Majesty's Island of Jamaica, in the
West Indies. (*ii*) Mr. William
Wood's preface to the octavo edition published in London, anno, 1776. (*iii*) A vindication of
the Conduct and Proceedings of
the English Government towards
the Spanish Nation in M.DC.LV.;
in reply to the misrepresentations
of some late historians; also some
account of the State of Jamaica, its
inhabitants and productions on its

surrender; by Bryan Edwards,
Esq. (*iv*) An Historical Account
of the Constitution of Jamaica;
drawn up in 1764 for the information of His Majesty's Ministers;
by His Excellency William Henry
Lyttleton, Esq., Governor and Com-
mander-in-Chief of that Island:
(*v*) An Abridgement of the Laws
of Jamaica: being an Alphabetical
Digest of all of the Public Acts of
Assembly now in force from the
thirty-second year of King Charles
II.; to the thirty-second of his present Majesty King George III., inclusive. *St. Jago de la Vega,* 1793

283—*DIODDEFIADAU miloedd lawer o
ddynion duon mewn caethiwed true-
nus yn Jamaica a lleoedd eraill;
yn cael eu gosod at ystyriaeth
ddifrifol y Cymry hawddgar, er
mwyn ceisio eu hennill i adael
suwgr, triagl a rum. Gan Gymro,
gelynol i bob gorthrech.
Caerfyrddin [*Carmarthen,* 1795 ?]

284—REMARKS on the late war in St·
Domingo, with observations on the
relative situation of Jamaica, and
other interesting subjects. By
Colonel Chalmers. *London,* 1803

285—AN ACCOUNT OF JAMAICA and its
inhabitants. By a gentleman long
resident in the West Indies [J. Ste-
wart]. *London,* 1808

The same. 2nd ed. *Kingston,* 1809
The same. A view of the Past and
Present state of the Island of Jamaica: with remarks on the nor-
mal and physical condition of the
Slaves and of the Abolition of Slavery in the Colonies. *Edinburgh,*
1823

The same. GEMÄLDE VON JAMAI-
CA VON J. STEWART. Aus dem
Englischen [A view of the Past and
Present State of the Island of Ja-
maica]. (Aus dem Ethnographis-
chen Archiv. besonders abge-
druckt). *Jena,* 1824

286—NOTICES RESPECTING JAMAICA in
1808-1809-1810. By Gilbert Mathi-
son. *London,* 1811

287—JAMAICA CONSIDERED in its present
state, political, financial and philosophical. By John Rippingham.
Kingston, 1817

288—HISTOIRE CIVILE ET COMMERCIALE de la Jamaïque; suivi du Tableau général des Possessions Anglaises et Françaises dans les Deux-Mondes, et de Réflexions commerciales et politiques relatives à la France et à l'Angleterre. Par M. Drouin-de-Bercy. *Paris,* 1818

289—A TOUR THROUGH THE ISLAND OF JAMAICA from the Western to the Eastern End, in the year 1823. By Cynric R. Williams. *London,* 1826

The same. 2nd ed. *London,* 1827

290—A PICTURESQUE TOUR of the Island of Jamaica, from Drawings made in the Years 1820 and 1821. By James Hakewill. *London,* 1825

291—JOURNAL OF A WEST INDIAN PROPRIETOR, kept during a residence in the Island of Jamaica. By Matthew Gregory Lewis, M.P. ["Monk Lewis"]. *London,* 1834

The same [revised ed.]. Journal of a Residence among the Negroes in the West Indies. New ed. *London,* 1861

292—A TWELVE-MONTHS RESIDENCE IN THE WEST INDIES, during the Transition from Slavery to Apprenticeship; with incidental notices of the state of Society, Prospects, and Natural Resources of Jamaica and other Islands. By R[ichard] R[obert] Madden, M.D. 2 vols. *London,* 1835

293—JAMAICA AS IT WAS, AS IT IS, AND AS IT MAY BE. Comprising interesting topics for absent Proprietors, Merchants, &c., and valuable hints to persons intending to emigrate to the Island: also an authentic narrative of the Negro Insurrection in 1831: with a faithful detail of the manners, customs and habits of the colonists, and a description of the country, climate, productions, &c., including an abridgment of the Slave Law. By a retired Military Officer. *London,* 1835

294—SKETCHES OF CHARACTER in illustration of the habits, occupation, and costume of the negro population, in the island of Jamaica, drawn after nature, and in lithography. By I. M. Belisario, *Kingston,* 1837

295—LETTERS FROM THE WEST INDIES: relating especially to . . Ja-maica. By Sylvester Hovey. *New York,* 1838

296—A JOURNAL OF A VOYAGE to, and residence in the Island of Jamaica, from 1801 to 1805, and subsequent events in England from 1805 to 1811. By Maria, Lady Nugent. 2 vols. *London,* 1839

297—THE PRESENT AND FUTURE STATE OF JAMAICA considered. By T. H. Milner. *London,* 1839

298—*WEST INDIES. Extracts from the Journal of John Candler whilst travelling in Jamaica. *London,* 1840

299—ILLUSTRATIONS OF JAMAICA, in a series of Views comprising the Principal Towns, Public Buildings, Estates and most Picturesque Scenery of the Island. By Joseph B. Kidd. (Coloured Copy). *London and Jamaica,* 1840

300—*LETTER TO HON. H. CLAY of Kentucky, relative to Jamaica. *New York,* 1840

301—JAMAICA (being the first part of) a series of letters written from Jamaica to a friend in England. *London,* 1842

302—JAMAICA: ITS PAST AND PRESENT STATE. By Rev. James M[urcell] Phillippo. *London,* 1843

303—DAGUERIAN EXCURSIONS IN JAMAICA: being a collection of Views of the most striking Scenery, Public Buildings, and other interesting objects taken on the spot with the Daguerreotype by Adolphe Duperly, and lithographed under his direction by the most eminent artists in Paris. *Kingston* n.d. [ab. 1844]

304—EARLY RECOLLECTIONS OF JAMAICA: with the particulars of an eventful passage Home *via* New York and Halifax, at the commencement of the American War in 1812 . . . By Rev. B. J. Vernon. *London,* 1848

*The same. *Oxford,* 1848

305—*REMARKS ON PRESENT STATE OF JAMAICA. By J. Maxwell, M.D. *London,* 1848

306—JAMAICA IN 1850, or the Effects of sixteen years of freedom on a slave colony. By John Bigelow. *New York and London,* 1851

307—JAMAICA AND THE AMERICANS [a lecture read by William Wemyss Anderson, Kingston, before the Colonial Literary Society, on 17th Jan., 1850.] *New York,* 1851

308—A DESCRIPTION AND HISTORY OF THE ISLAND OF JAMAICA comprising an account of its soil, climate and productions, shewing its value and importance as an agricultural country, and a desirable place of residence for certain classes of settlers. Reprinted (it is believ.d for the first time) from the great work, "An Account of America, or the New World," by John Ogilby, Esq., Master of the Revels in Ireland. First published in the year 1671. With preliminary chapter and notes, to connect the work with our own times. By William Wemyss Anderson. [Map]. *Kingston,* 1851

309— *OUR WEST INDIAN COLONIES. By H. B. Evans. *Jamaica,* 1855

310—JAMAICA. Its Existing Condition with a few suggestions for its amelioration. As submitted to the Right Hon. H. M. Secretary of State for the Colonies. [By Leonard Rowe Valpy and others]. *London,* 1856

311—AN ABRIDGED HISTORY OF JAMAICA. From the discovery of the island in 1594 to the termination of the Duke of Manchester's Government in 1827. To which is added a brief retrospect of events up to the present time. By James Otway Clerk. *Falmouth,* 1859

312—LIGHTS AND SHADOWS OF JAMAICA HISTORY. Being three lectures delivered in aid of the Mission Schools of the Colony. By Richard Hill. To which is added an appendix with Ford and Gall's map of the island. *Kingston,* 1859

313—* ABOUT JAMAICA. By R. Emery, 1859

314—REMINISCENCES OF A SCOTTISH GENTLEMAN commencing in 1787. By "Philo Scotus" [Philip Barrington Ainslie]. *London,* 1861

315—*LETTER WITH ILLUSTRATIVE DOCUMENTS on the condition of Jamaica and an Explanatory Statement. By E. Bean Underhill, 1865

316—THE PROBLEM OF JAMAICA; The Jeopardy of Jamaica. Reprinted from the Eclectic Review. [ab. 1865]

317—JAMAICA IN 1866. A Narrative of a tour through the Island with remarks on its social, educational, and industrial condition. By Thomas Harvey and William Brewin. *London,* 1867

318—PAPERS ON JAMAICA : Descriptive of its Soil, Climate, Productions and Physical Aspect; selected and arranged for the information of intending Colonists. *Kingston,* 1867

319--EIGHT CHAPTERS IN THE HISTORY OF JAMAICA, from A.D. 1508 to A.D. 1680, illustrating the settlement of the Jews in the island. By Richard Hill. Published in aid of the funds of the Hebrew Benevolent Society. *Kingston,* 1868

320—LETTERS FROM JAMAICA. The Land of Streams and Woods. By Charles Rampini. *Edinburgh,* 1873

321—TO JAMAICA AND BACK. By Sir Sibbald David Scott, Bart. *London,* 1876

322—WHAT I HAVE SEEN IN JAMAICA, A Lecture by Florence L. Marsh, delivered in Kingston and other Towns in Jamaica, during 1876 . . *Kingston,* 1876

323—JAMAICA, PART OF HER HISTORY, Climate, Resources and general aspect. A lecture by Francilla Nash, delivered at the Judges Hall, Centennial Exhibition, Philadelphia, August 29th, 1876. *New York,* 1877

324—JAMAICA. CORRESPONDENT'S LETTER TO LONDON "STANDARD," October, 16th. 1877

325—JAMAICA : NOW AND FIFTEEN YEARS SINCE. A paper read before the Royal Colonial Institute on April 29th, 1880, by Sir Anthony Musgrave, K.C.M.G., Governor of Jamaica. *Kingston,* 1880

326—*WARMER ISLANDS : A tour to Madiera and Jamaica. *London,* 1881

327—JAMAICA : ITS GOVERNMENT AND ITS PEOPLE. By Dr. J[ames] C[ecil] Phillippo, M.D., L.R.C.S., Ed. *Kingston,* 1883

328—*THOUGHTS ON THE CONDITION OF JAMAICA ; and what the Government should undertake, to arrest the fearful decadence which each new year foreshadows. By Nil Desperandum. *Kingston,*   1887

329—PICTURESQUE JAMAICA: in ten parts [5 only published]. By V. P. Parkhurst. *Kingston,*   1887

330—JAMAICA'S JUBILEE or what we are and what we hope to be; by five of themselves [Rev. R. Gordon; W. F. Bailey; Rev. S. J. Washington; J. H. Reid; R. Dingwall]. *London,*   1888

331—UNTRODDEN JAMAICA. By Herbert T. Thomas. Illustrated by the author. *Kingston,*   1890

332—THE NEW JAMAICA, describing the island, explaining its conditions of life and growth and discussing its mercantile relations and potential importance: adding somewhat in relation to those matters which directly interest the tourist and health-seeker. By Edgar Mayhew Bacon and Eugene Murray Aaron, Ph. D. Illustrated by the authors after original sketches and from photographs taken by Dr. Jas. Johnston and others. Map. *New York and Kingston,*   1890

333—THE JUBILEE REIGN OF HER MOST GRACIOUS MAJESTY QUEEN VICTORIA IN JAMAICA. Being a complete account of the principal and important events which occurred in Jamaica during the fifty years reign of Her Most Gracious Majesty Queen Victoria, * * * and also a full and complete Account of the Jubilee Rejoicings in Jamaica in 1887. By W. A. Feurtado. *Kingston,*   1890

334—ADVENTURES AMIDST THE EQUATORIAL FORESTS AND RIVERS OF SOUTH AMERICA; also in the West Indies and the Wilds of Florida, to which is added " Jamaica Re-visited." By Villiers Stuart, of Dromana. With many illustrations and Maps. *London,*   1891.

335—JAMAICA IN 1895, A Handbook of Information for intending Settlers and others. (Institute of Jamaica). [Edited by Frank Cundall.] *Kingston,*   1895
   The same in 1896   1896
   The same in 1897   1897

The same in 1901. A Handbook of Information for intending settlers with Notes for Visitors. 1901

336—ILLUSTRATED SOUVENIR ALBUM OF JAMAICA. Containing views of the Island and Representative Business Houses. *Toronto,*   1895

337—JAMAICA QUEEN OF THE CARIB SEA. By Ethel Maud Symmonette. *Jamaica,*   1895

338—PHOTOGRAPHS OF THE PRINCIPAL BRIDGES erected in the island from 1890 to 1895. Sir Henry Arthur Blake, K.C.M.G., Governor. [Hon. V. G. Bell, M.I.C.E., Director of Public Works]. *Kingston,*   1895

339—ET BESOG PAA JAMAIKA. [by] Dr. Hans Reusch. *Kristiania,*   1895

340—BUCKRA LAND. Two weeks in Jamaica. Details of a voyage to the West Indies, day by day, and a Tour of Jamaica, step by step. By C. W. Willis (''Allan Eric''). With Appendix. 2nd ed. *Boston,*   1897

341—MY WINTER IN THE TROPICS. By General John Corson Smith. *Chicago,*   1897

342—*IM FLUGE DURCH JAMAICA und Cuba. Von Dr. H. Paasch. *Stuttgart,*   1900

343—A PEEP AT JAMAICA AND ITS PEOPLE. By Mrs. T. B. Butcher. With preface by Rev. Geo. Sykes. *London,*   1902

IV. GUIDE BOOKS.

344—THE TOURISTS' GUIDE to the chief Towns and Villages of the island of Jamaica. To which are appended several scientific synopses and other valuable information connected with the Natural History of the island. Compiled by G. Arnaboldi. *Kingston,*   1852

345—HANDY GUIDE TO JAMAICA, 1889. Containing information useful to Tourists and Residents, a short sketch of some incidents in the History of the Colony, a collection of Local Proverbs and other interesting matter. By Aston W. Gardner. *Jamaica,*   1889

346—A TOURISTS' GUIDE TO THE PARISHES OF JAMAICA togther with an account descriptive of the Jamaica Exhibition 1891: being a supplement to DeSouza's edition of the Jamaica Commercial Almanack and Pocket Journal. *Kingston*, [1891]

347— WHAT TO SEE! WHERE TO SEE! AND HOW TO SEE IT! The Tourists' Guide to Kingston and the parishes of Jamaica. By Rambler. *Kingston*, n.d. [after 1891]

348—TOURIST GUIDE TO THE ISLAND OF JAMAICA. Specially compiled for Aston W. Gardner & Co. *Kingston*, 1893

349 — RAYMOND AND WHITCOMB'S TOURS. Two Tours Southward through Florida to the Island of Jamaica. *Boston*, 1897

350—JAMAICA GUIDE (illustrated) containing a description of everything relating to Jamaica of which the visitor or resident may desire information : including its history, inhabitants, government, resources, and places of interest to travellers. By James H. Stark. Fully illustrated with maps, engravings, and photo-prints. *Boston* [U. S. A.] *and London*, [1898]

The same. 2nd ed. *Boston*, 1902

351—JAMAICA AND THE IMPERIAL DIRECT WEST INDIA MAIL SERVICE. By Thomas Rhodes. *London*, 1901

352—SIDE TRIPS IN JAMAICA. By Mary F. Bradford. Illustrated. *Boston*, [1901]

V. BIOGRAPHY.

353— A VINDICATION OF THE LATE GOVERNOR, [Admiral Lord Archibald Hamilton] and Council of Jamaica. Occasioned by a letter in the St. James's Post on the 23rd of July last, as from Bath in a letter to ——. *London*, 1716

354—AN ANSWER TO AN ANONYMOUS LIBEL entitled Articles exhibited against Lord Archibald Hamilton, late Governor of Jamaica : with sundry depositions and proofs relating to the same. *London*, 1718

355—A GENERAL HISTORY OF THE PYRATES : [chiefly those of the West Indies : also list of their names.] By Capt. Charles Johnson. 2nd ed. with considerable additions. . . . With the remarkable Actions and Adventures of the Two Female Pyrates, Mary Read and Anne Bonnie. [With illustrations.] *London*, 1724

356—A TRUE AND FAITHFUL NARRATIVE OF THE LIFE AND ACTIONS OF JOHN ONEBY, ESQ., commonly called Major Oneby ; . . giving an account of his birth, parentage and education. Of his killing . . Lieut. Trolley in Jamaica . . . *London*, n.d. [ab. 1727]

357—A FAITHFUL NARRATIVE OF THE UNFORTUNATE ADVENTURES OF CHARLES CARTWRIGHT, M. D., who in his voyage to Jamaica was taken by a Spanish Privateer and carried into St. Sebastian. His hard usage there and wonderful escape from thence. . . *London*, 1741

358—*HISTORY OF MISS KATTY N——, containing a faithful and particular relation of her Amours, Adventures and various turns of Fortune in Scotland, Ireland, Jamaica and England, written by herself. [ab. 1750]

359—THE PEREGRINATIONS OF JEREMIAH GRANT, ESQ., the West Indian [of Jamaica]. *London*, 1763

360 –*MEMOIRS OF EDWARD MARCUS DESPARD. By James Bannantine, 1799

361 –*THE LIFE AND EXPLOITS OF MANSONY. COMMONLY CALLED THREE-FINGER'D JACK, the terror of Jamaica. *Somers Town*, [1800]

362—THE HISTORY OF THREE-FINGER'D JACK, the terror of Jamaica. . . being the history on which is founded the pantominical Drama of " Obi, or Three-finger'd Jack" . . . to which is added a Description of the Drama, and some of the most favourite Songs, selected from the best authorities. *London*. n. d.

363—THE LIFE AND ADVENTURES OF THREE-FINGERED JACK, the Terror of Jamaica. Hodgson's edition. *London*. n. d.

364 –A SHORT VIEW OF THE LIFE AND CHARACTER OF LIEUT. GENERAL VILLETTES, late Lieut.-Governor and Commander of the Forces in Jamaica. By Thomas Bowdler, F.R.S. & S.A. . . . *Bath and London*, 1815

The same. London, 1815

364a—A Memoir of Major-General Sir Robert Rollo Gillespie. *London,* 1816

365—The Experienced Angler . . . By Col. Robert Venables. [With Memoir of Col. Robert Venables]. *London,* 1825

366—Memoir of the late William Wright, M.D., with extracts from his correspondence, and a selection of his papers on Medical and Botanical Subjects [concerning Jamaica.] *Edinburgh and London,* 1828

367—The Youthful Female Missionary. A Memoir of Mary Ann Hutchins, wife of the Rev. John Hutchins, Baptist Missionary, Savanna-la-Mar, Jamaica, and daughter of the Rev. T. Middleditch ot Ipswich. Compiled, chiefly from her own correspondence, by her father, Rev. T. Middleditch. *London and Ipswich,* 1839

368—The Farewell Addresses of the Inhabitants of Jamaica to the Right Honourable Sir Charles Theophilus Metcalfe, Baronet, &c., Governor of the Island. *Kingston,* 1842

369—A View of the Formation, Discipline and Economy of Armies. By Robert Jackson, M.D. 3rd ed. revised with a memoir of his life and services drawn up from his own papers, and the communications of his survivors. *London,* 1845

370—*Memoir of William Knibb, son of the Rev. W. Knibb, Missionary, who died at the Refuge, near Falmouth, Jamaica; with an address to the coloured children. By Dr. James Hoby. *London.* n. d. [aft. 1845]

371—Memoir of William Knibb, Missionary in Jamaica. By John Howard Hinton, M.A. 8vo. *London,* 1847

The same. 1849

372—Memoir of Thomas Burchell, twenty-two years a Missionary in Jamaica. By his brother William Fitz-er Burchell. *London,* 1849

373—*The Jamaica Missionary : a Memoir of William Knibb. By George E. Sargeant. *London,* [ab. 1849]

374—Memoir of the late Rev. Thomas P. Callender, Missionary to Jamaica. With a selection of his Pulpit Discourses. [with portrait]. *Edinburgh and London,* 1850

375—The Life and Correspondence of Charles, Lord Metcalfe, late Governor-General of India, Governor of Jamaica and Governor-General of Canada. From unpublished letters and journals preserved by himself, his family and his friends. 2 vols. By Sir John William Kaye. *London,* 1854

The same. New and revised ed. *London,* 1858

376—The Story of my Girlhood. By Mrs. Henry Lynch. *London,* 1857

377—The Gospel to the Africans : a narrative of the Life and Labours of the Rev. William Jameson in Jamaica and Old Calabar, by his brother-in-law, Rev. Alexander Robb, D.D. [Portrait]. 3rd thousand. *Edinburgh and London,* [1861]

378—Addresses to His Excellency Edward John Eyre, &c., 1865, 1866. [*Jamaica*], 1866

379—Personal Recollections of the Hon. George William Gordon, late of Jamaica. By Rev. Duncan Fletcher. [portrait]. *London,* 1867

The same [new title as follows]. The Life of the Honourable George W. Gordon, the Martyr of Jamaica. 2nd ed., enlarged and improved. *London,* 1867

380—The Life of Edward John Eyre, late Governor of Jamaica. By Hamilton Hume. *London,* 1867

381—Letters and Journals of James 8th Earl of Elgin, Governor of Jamaica, Governor-General of Canada, Envoy to China, Viceroy of India. Edited by Theodore Walrond, C.B., with a preface by Arthur Penrhyn Stanley, D.D., Dean of Westminster. *London,* 1872

382—Brief Memorial of the late Rev. James Watson, Missionary in Jamaica from A.D. 1827 till 1868. [*Edinburgh,* ?1873]

383 —Political Life of the Hon. Charles Hamilton Jackson. A sketch of the Political History of Jamaica for the past thirty years. By A[ugustus] C[onstantine] Sinclair. *Kingston,* 1878

384—Life of James Mursell Phillippo, Missionary in Jamaica. By Edward Bean Underhill, LL.D., *London,* 1881

384a—Address presented to His Excellency Sir Anthony Musgrave, K.C.M.G., on his retiring from the Government of Jamaica, together with His Excellency's reply. 1883

385—Thirty-eight Years' Mission Life in Jamaica. A Brief Sketch of the Rev. Warrand Carlile, Missionary at Brownsville. By one of his sons [Rev. Gavin Carlile]. *London,* 1884

386—In Memoriam. Dr. E. J. Waring, C.I.E. n.d. [ab. 1891]

387—In Memoriam of Rev. J. M. Denniston, M.A., who departed to be at home with the Lord, June 13th, 1895. n.d. [?1895]

388—William Knibb; Missionary in Jamaica. A Memoir. By [M.E.] Mrs. John James Smith. With an introduction by Rev. J. G. Greenhough, M.A. *London,* 1896

389—James John Bowrey. In Memoriam : 1845-1897. [With prefatory words by Rev. James Watson], n.d. [1898]

390 - William and Louisa Anderson. A Record of their life and work in Jamaica and old Calabar. By William Marwick. With portraits and maps. *Edinburgh,* 1897

391 —Obituary Notice of Sir Edward Newton, M.A., K.C.M.G., F.L.S. Reprint from "The Ibis", 1897

392—Grant Allen, 1848-1899. An address delivered at Woking on October 27, 1899 by Frederic Harrison. *Privately printed.* 1899

VI. i. Zoology.

393—Jamaica Birds described by Dr. Anthony Robinson. 3 vols. MSS. [bef. 1768]

394—*Contribution to Conchology: conducted by C. B. Adams, Profes-

sor of Zoology in Amhurst College Mass. Vol. 1. October 1849—November 1852. *New York,* 1849-1852

395 —*Contributions to the Natural History of the Shark. By Richard Hill. *Spanish Town,* 1850

396—A Naturalist's Sojourn in Jamaica. By Philip Henry Gosse, F.R.S., and Richard Hill, Cor. M.Z.S., Lond. *London,* 1851

397—*Contribution to Conchology. By Edward Chitty. *Kingston,* 1853

398—The Birds of Jamaica. By Philip Henry Gosse, F.R.S., assisted by Richard Hill. *London,* 1847

The same. Illustrations of the Birds of Jamaica. *London,* 1849

399—Beiträge zur Schmetterlings-Fauna von Jamaica. By H. B. Moeschler. (No title.) 1886

400—Exhibition of Two Skulls from a cave in Jamaica. By Prof. W. H. Flower, C.B., F.R.S. Reprinted from " Journal of the Anthropological Institute," *London,* 1890

401—The Colours of Insects. By T. D. A. Cockerell. Reprinted from the " Entomologist." *London,* 1891

402—A Provisional List of the Fishes of Jamaica. (Bulletin No. 1 of the Institute of Jamaia.) By Theodore D. A. Cockerell, F.Z.S., F.E.S. *Kingston,* 1892

403—New Jamaica Tachinidæ. By C. H. Tyler Townsend. Reprinted from " Entomoligical News" *London,* 1892

404—Two new species of Pulvinaria from Jamaica. By Theodore D. A. Cockerell, F. Z. S., F. E. S. Reprinted from " Transactions of the Entomological Society." *London,* 1893

405—On the genus Alicia (Cladactis), with an anatomical description of A. costæ, Panc. By J. E. Duerden. Reprinted from the " Annals and Magazine of Natural History." *London,* 1895

406—Johns Hopkins University Circulars, 1897. Notes from the Biological Laboratory. *Baltimore,* 1897

407—The Actiniarian Family Alicidæ. By J. E. Duerden. Reprinted from the "Annals and Magazine of Natural History." *Londo*,   1897

408—OBSERVATIONS ON THE GENUS BARRETTIA WOODWARD, with descriptions of two new species. By R. P. Whitfield. Reprinted from "Bulletin of the American Museum of Natural History." *New York*, 1897

409—DESCRIPTIONS OF SPECIES OF RUDISTÆ from the Cretaceous Rocks of Jamaica, W. I., collected and presented by Mr. F. C. Nicholas. By R. P. Whitfield. Reprinted from "Bulletin of the American Museum of Natural History." *New York*, 1897

410—A NEW MARINE HYDROMETRID. By George H. Carpenter. B.Sc., F.E.S. Reprinted from the "Entomologist's Monthly Magazine," *London*,   1898.

411—THE GEOGRAPHICAL DISTRIBUTION OF THE ACTINIARIA OF JAMAICA. By J. E. Duerden,   Reprinted from "Natural Science." *London*, 1898.

412—TROCHOPUS AND RHAGOVELLA. By George H. Carpenter, B.Sc. Reprinted from the "Entomologist's Monthly Magazine." *London*, 1898

412a —A NEW SPECIES OF SPHÆNOGONA FROM JAMAICA. By Percy J. Lathy. Reprinted from the "Entomologist's Monthly Magazine," *London*, 1898

413—ON THE RELATIONS OF CERTAIN STICHODACTYLINÆ TO THE MADREPORARIA.   By J. E. Duerden, A.R.C. Sc. (Lond).   (Communicated by Prof. G. B. Howes, F.R. S. Sec. L.S.). Extracted from the "Linnean Society's Journal—Zoology, Vol. XXVI. *London*, 1898

VI. ii. BOTANY.

414—THE INDIAN NECTAR, or a Discourse concerning Chocolata : Wherein the nature of the Cacaonut, and other Ingredients of that composition is examined, and stated according to the Judgment and experience of the Indians, and Spanish Writers, who lived in the Indies and others ; with sundry additional observations made in England. . . By Henry Stubb, formerly of Ch. Ch. in Oxon, Physician for His Ma-

jesty, and the Right Honourable Thomas Lord Windsor in the Island of Jamaica in the West Indies. *London*,   1662.

415—CATALOGUS PLANTARUM quae in Insula Jamaica . . . Maderae, Barbados, Nieves, et Sancti Christophori nascuntur . . Aùtore Hans Sloane, M.D. *London*, 1696

416—THE CIVIL AND NATURAL HISTORY OF JAMAICA. In three parts. Containing, (i.) an accurate description of that island, its situation and soil; with a brief account of its former and present state, government, revenues, produce and trade. (ii.) an history of the natural productions, including the various sorts of native fossils, perfect and imperfect vegetables, quadrupeds, birds, fishes, reptiles and insects ; with their properties and uses in mechanics, diet and physic. (iii) an account of the nature of climates in general, and their different effects upon the human body ; with a detail of the diseases arising from this source, particularly within the tropics. In three dissertations.   The whole illustrated with fifty copper plates. By Patrick Browne, M.D. *London*, 1756

The same. 2nd ed. [Part I. only, without illustrations.]   *London*, 1769

The same. Illustrated with forty-nine copper plates ; in which the most curious productions are represented of their natural sizes, and delineated immediately from the objects, by George Dionysius Ehret. There are now added complete Linnæan Indexes and a large and accurate map of the island. 3rd ed. *London*,   1789

417—SELECTARUM STIRPIUM AMERICANARUM HISTORIA in qua ad Linnæanum systema determinatæ descriptæque sistuntur plantae illæ quas in insulis Martinica, Jamaica, Domingo, aliisque, et in Vicinæ continentis parte observavit Rariores : adjectis inconibus in solo natali delineatis. Nicolai Josephi Jacquin. *Vindobonæ*,   1763

The same. Vindobonæ,   circ. 1780

The same. Manhemii,   1788

418—Description of Jamaica Fauna and Flora. By Dr. Anthony Robinson. Manuscripts and Drawings. 1 vol., Index containing also various figures and maps. 1 vol., General Index and descriptions of Plants. 1 vol., Description of Plants and Animals. 1 vol., Description of Plants and Birds. 1 vol., Description of Plants, Animals and Miscellaneous matter. [The above are copies made under the direction of Robert Long from the original ms. of Dr. Robinson]. 1 vol. containing 455 plates by Dr. Robinson. 1 vol. containing 25 plates by A. Dupont. 5 vols. ms. and 2 vols. drawings. [Jamaica], n.d. [bef. 1768]

419—Nova Genera et species plantarum seu Prodromus descriptiorium vegetabilium, maximam partem incognitorum quae sub itinere in Indiam occidentalem annis 1783-87 digessit. Olof Swartz. Holmiae, 1788

420—*Intradestal. innehallande anmarkningar om Vestindien, hållet inför Kongl. Vetenskaps Academien den 18 Martii, 1789. Olof Swartz. Stockholm, 1790

421—Obrervationes botanicae quibus plantae Indiae occidentalis aliaeque systematis vegetabilium ed xiv. illustrantur earumque characteres passim emendatur. Olof Swartz. Erlangae, 1791

422— *Catalogue of Plants, exotic and indigenous, in the Botanical Garden, Jamaica, 1792. · By Thomas Dancer. St. Jago de la Vega, [1792]

423—*Hortus Eastensis or a Catalogue of Exotic Plants in the Garden of Hinton East, Esq., in the mountains of Liguanea at the time of his decease. By Arthur Broughton. Kingston, 1792

*The same. Hortus Eastensis, or a Catalogue of Exotic Plants cultivated in the Botanic Gardens in the mountains of Liguanea. By Arthur Broughton. St. Jago de la Vega. 1794

424—Icones plantarum incognitarum, quas in India occidentali detexit atque delineavit. Olof Swartz. Erlangae, 1794 & 1800

425—Flora Indiae occidentalis aucta atque illustrata sive descriptiones plantarum in Prodromo recensitarum. Olof Swartz. Erlangae, 1797-1806

426—Hortus Americanus; containing an account of the trees, shrubs and other vegetable productions of South America and the West India Islands, and particularly of the island of Jamaica; interspersed with many curious and useful observations respecting their uses in medicine, diet and mechanics. By Dr. Henry Barham. To which are added a Linnean Index, &c. Kingston, 1794

427—Some Observations respecting the Botanical Garden [at Bath]. By Thomas Dancer. Jamaica, 1804

428—Sketches towards a Hortus Botanicus Americanus; or Coloured Plates [with a Catalogue and concise and familiar descriptions of many species] of new and valuable plants of the West Indies and North and South America. Also of several others, natives of Africa and the East Indies. Arranged after the Linnean System. By W[illiam] J[owit] Titford, M.D. With a . . . glossary of terms and a general index. London, 1811

429—Hortus Jamaicensis. Botanical Description according to the Linnean System and an account of the virtues, &c., of its Indigenous Plants hitherto known, as also of the most useful exotics. By John Lunan. Compiled from the best authorities and alphabetically arranged. 2 vols. Jamaica, 1814

430—* Hortus Eastensis. By James Wiles. 1826

431—The Flora of Jamaica. A description of the plants of that Island arranged according to the natural orders. With an appendix containing an enumeration of the genera according to the Linnean System, and an essay on the Geographical Distribution of the species. By James Macfadyen, M.D. 2 vols. Vol. 1. Rannuculaceæ-Leguminosæ. Vol. 2. Rosaceæ-Rubiaceæ. London, 1837

432—Description of the Nelumbium Jamaicense, the Jamaica Water Bean. By James Macfadyen, M.D., F.L.S., [with plates]. *Kingston,* 1847

433—*Account of the cultivation of the *Victoria regia* in the garden of Edward Chitty. *Kingston,* 1852

434—Flora of the British West Indian Islands. By A. H. R. Grisebach. *London,* 1864

435—Department of Public Gardens and Plantations, Jamaica. Circulars, 1880, 1881, 1882. *Kingston,* 1880-1882

436—A Hand-List of the Jamaica Ferns and their allies. By G. S. Jenman. 2nd ed. *Demerara.* 1881

437—Notes on Liberian Coffee. By D. Morris. *Kingston,* 1881

438—Correspondence relating to the Aphis Blight on Sugar Cane in Jamaica. By D. Morris. *Kingston,* 1882

439—Report upon the Forests of Jamaica. By E. D. M. Hooper, Esq. *London,* 1886

440—Sisal Hemp: its adaptation to Jamaica, planting, working, general management and final out-turn. By Daniel J. Stoddart. *Kingston,* 1886

441—Bulletin of the Botanical Department, containing No. 1, April, 1887 to Dec., 1901. *Jamaica, 1887-1901*

442—Disease of Colocasia in Jamaica. By George Massee: with an introductory note by D. Morris, M.A , F.L.S. Extracted from " Linnean Society's Journal, Botany " *London,* 1887

443—Department of Public Gardens and Plantations. Memorandum concerning Cocoes. *Kingston, 1887*

444—A Jubilee Guide on Gardening in Jamaica. Twenty years' Experience. [By William Speck]. *Kingston,* 1887

The same. A Guide to Gardening in Jamaica. 2nd ed., illustrated. Twenty-five years experience. By William Speck. *Jamaica, 1891*

445—Economic Plants. An index to Economic Products of the Vegetable Kingdom in Jamaica. By William Fawcett, B.Sc., F.L.S. *Kingston,* 189-

446—A Provisional List of the Indigenous and Naturalised Flowering Plants of Jamaica. By William Fawcett, B.Sc., F.L.S. *Kingston,* 1893

447— Castleton Gardens. Notes on the most interesting plants. Being parts 10, 11 and 12 of vol. 1 (new series) of the " Bulletin of the Botanical Department, Jamaica. By William Fawcett, B.Sc., F.L.S. *Kingston,* 1895

VI. iii. Geology.

448—Report on the Copper Veins of the Parish of Portland, Jamaica. By Lucas Barrett, F.L.S., F.G.S. *London,* 1861

449—A Notice of the Geology of Jamaica especially with reference to the District of Clarendon; with descriptions of the Cretaceous, Eocene and Miocene Corals of the island. By P. Martin Duncan, M.B., Sec. Geo. Soc., and G. P. Wall, F.G.S., late of the Geological Survey of the West Indies. *Lond n,* 1864

450—Manuscript Catalogue of the Rocks, Fossils and Minerals collected in the Official Geological Survey of Jamaica 1859-66, in the Museum of the Institute of Jamaica, Kingston. Compiled by Henry Vendryes, 1866

451—Memoirs of the Geological Survey. Reports on the Geology of Jamaica or Part ii. of the West Indian Survey. By James G. Sawkins, F.G.S. With contributions from G. P. Wall, F.G.S., Lucas Barrett, Arthur Lennox, F.G.S., and C. B. Brown. With an appendix by Robert Etheridge, F.G.S., F.R.S.E. [Map.] *London,* 1866

453—On the Geology of Jamaica; and On Mining in Jamaica. By Rev. H[orace] Scotland. *Kingston,* 1889

454—The Geology and Physical Geography of Jamaica: Study of a type of Antillean Development. By Robert T Hill. Based upon surveys made for Alexander Agassiz. With an appendix of some Cretaceous and Eocene Corals from Jamaica, by T

Wayland Vaughan. With 41 plates. (Bulletin of the Museum of Comparative Geology at Havard College, vol. xxxiv). *Cambridge, Mass.,* 1899

VI. iv. CLIMATE.

455—*A DISCOURSE of the State of Health of Jamaica, with a provision therefore calculated from the air, the place and the water ; the customs and manners of living, &c. *London,* 1679

456—THE STATE AND PROSPECTS OF JAMAICA ; with appended remarks on its advantages for the cure of Pulmonary diseases. and suggestions to invalids and others going to that colony. By Rev. David King, LL.D. *London and Edinburgh,* 1850

457—THE CLIMATE OF JAMAICA, By Dr. J[ames] C[ecil] Phillippo, M.D., L.R.C.S., Ed. *London,* 1876

458—JAMAICA METEOROLOGICAL OBSERVATIONS. 3 Vols. : containing Reports from June, 1881, to Feb., 1902 inclusive. By Maxwell Hall. *Jamaica,* 1889, 1896 and 1902

459—THE RAINFALL OF JAMAICA. Thirteen maps showing the average Rainfall in each month and during the year with explanatory text. By Maxwell Hall, M.A., F.R.A.S., F.R.M.S. *Kingston,* 1892

460—THE KINGSTON ANEMOMETER or Record of Observations upon the the hourly velocity and force of the wind throughout the three years, March, 1892 to Feb. 1895. With other Notes, including tables and diagrams. [By J. F. Brennan.] *Kingston,* 1896

VII. HYGIENE AND MEDICINE.

461—*AN ESSAY on the Bilious or Yellow Fever of Jamaica, collected from the MS. of a late Surgeon, by Charles Blicke. 1772

462—*OBSERVATIONS on the Dysentery of the West Indies, with a new and successful method of treating it. By Benjamin Moseley. *Jamaica.*

The same. London reprint, 1781

463—A SHORT DISSERTATION on the Jamaica Bath Waters, to which is prefixed an introduction concern-

ing mineral waters in general, shewing the methods of examining them, and accertaining their contents. By Thomas Dancer, M.D. *Kingston,* 1784

464—OBSERVATIONS on the diseases of the Army in Jamaica, and on the best means of preserving the health of Europeans in that climate. By John Hunter, M.D. [d. 1809]. *London,* 1788

The same. BEMERKUNGEN UBER DIE KRANKHEITEN der Truppen in Jamaica, und die besten Mittel die Gesundheit der Europaer in dem dasigen Klima zu erhalten . . . aus dem Englischen von John Hunter, M.D., übersetzt. *Leipzig,* 1792

465—*A TREATISE ON THE FEVERS OF JAMAICA, with some observations on the Intermitting Fever of America and an appendix containing some hints on the means of preserving the health of soldiers in hot climates. By Robert Jackson, M.D. *London,* 1791

The same. Philadelphia, 1795

The same. ROBERT JACKSON UBER DIB FIEBER in Jamaika ; aus dem Englischen übersetzt mit Anmerkungen und Zusätzen von Kurt Sprengel. *Leipzig,* 1796

The same. RICERCHE SULL'INDOLE E SULLA CURA DELLA FEBBRE GIALLA, coll' aggiunta di un saggio sulla febbre gialla della Giamaica, tradotto dall'Inglese [by] Giovanni Maria Zecchinelli. *Padova,* 1805

466—THE MEDICAL ASSISTANT or Jamaica Practice of Physic designed chiefly for the use of families and plantations. By Thomas Dancer, M.D. *Kingston,* 1801

The same. 2nd ed. [with author's manuscript notes]. *St. Jago de la Vega,* 1809

The same. 3rd ed. corrected by himself, with much additional matter. *London and Kingston,* 1819

* *The same.* American ed.

467—A ROWLAND FOR AN OLIVER : or a Jamaica Review of the Edinburgh Reviewers [By Thomas Dancer ; being a defence of his work, entitled "The Medical Assistant."] *St. Jago de la Vega,*   1809

468—* Port Henderson and its Bath, its Properties and Virtues. By Thomas Dancer.

469—A Treatise on the Diseases of the Negroes as they occur in the island of Jamaica, with observations on the Country Remedies. By James Thomson, M.D. *Jamaica,*   1820

470—Observations on Yaws and its influence in originating Leprosy: also observations on Acute Traumatic Tetanus and Tetanus Infantum. By James Maxwell, M.D.   [Prize Essay.] *Edinburgh and London,*   1839

471—*A Letter to the Hon. Hector Mitchell on the proposed erection of a new Lunatic Asylum. from Edward Nathaniel Bancroft,   1839

472—*A Letter to the Hon. Hector Mitchell rspresenting the Total Unfitness of the present Asylum for Lunatics, and the urgent necessity for building a new Lunatic Asylum in a proper situation.   By E. N. Bancroft.   1840

473—Practical Treatise on the bilious remittent Fever; its causes and effects, with illustrative tables and cases on the temperature of the system in the febrile diseases of Jamaica. By William Arnold, M.D. *London,*   1840

474—Copies or Extracts of Despatches and other Documents relating to the outbreak of the Cholera in the Island of Jamaica, and respecting any applications made to Her Majesty's Government for the adoption of measures to meet the difficulties thus brought upon the Colony. *London,*   1851

475—Report on the Cholera in Jamaica by Dr. Gavin Milroy. [With appendix. and maps]. *London,* 1853

476—Statistical Report of the Epidemic Cholera in Jamaica.   By John Parkin, M.D. *London,*   1852

477—Report by the Central Board of Health of Jamaica: (with plan of the Town of St. Jago de la Vega.) *Spanish Town,*   1852

—*The same.* [With appendix]. *Spanish Town,*   1852

478—Notification of the Central Board of Health [of Jamaica] [concerning cholera]. Drawn up and presented by the members of the Standing Committee for Kingston. *London,*   1854

479—Tables and Tracts connected with the Valuation whether of Annuities or Assurances contingent on the duration of Life, or of Sums and Annuities certain.   With various formulæ and incidental notices.   To establish on some permanent and authoratative basis, a comprehensive system for the determining of pecuniary values contingent on the duration of human life among acclimated subjects as well in the island of Jamaica as in other British West India Possessions. By J. Marshall. *Kingston.*   1855

480—Observations on the outbreak of Yellow Fever among the Troops at Newcastle, Jamaica, in the latter part of 1856.   By Robert Lawson, Deputy Inspector-General of Army Hospitals and Principal Medical Officer at Jamaica. Printed for private circulation. n.d. [?*London*], ab. 1856

481—Observation on Tubercular and Anæsthetic Leprosy, as they occur in Jamaica. By Alexander Fiddes, L.R.C.S., Edin.   (Reprinted from the Edinburgh Medical Journal, June, 1857.). *Edinburgh,*   1857

482—The Evidence of the present Sanitary condition of Jamaica, and its great need of medical and surgical practitioners. Collected and published by the Society for promoting sanitary, educational, social and moral remedial measures, Feby. 1858. [Compiled by the Rev. B. Bayly Kingdon]. *Kingston,*   [1858]

483—Rules and Regulations to be observed by Patients, Officers and Visitors in the Public Hospital, Jamaica. n.d.

484—Official Documents on the case of Ann Pratt, the reputed authoress of a certain pamphlet entitled " Seven Months in the Kingston

Lunatic Asylum and what I saw there." *Kingston,* 1860

485—OFFICIAL DOCUMENTS published by command of His Excellency Charles Henry Darling, Esq., Governor of Jamaica, on the case of Ann Pratt, reviewed and answered in a letter to His Excellency the Governor. *Kingston,* 1860

486—REPORT of the Commissioners appointed to enquire into the management of the Public Hospital and Lunatic Asylum, and the evidence upon which such report is founded [presented to the House of Assembly, Nov. 1861]. To which is added an appendix of papers referred to in the evidence given before the above Commission. *Jamaica,* 1862

486a—LEPROSY. Abstracts of Replies to Interrogatories prepared by the Leprosy Committee of the Royal College of Physicians. With Appendix. *London,* 1864

487—THE REPORT of the ordinary and resident Medical Officers and the Annual Report of the Inspector and Director of the Public Hospital for 1864 with the reply of the ordinary medical officers thereto. The letter of Alexander Fiddes, Esq., F.R.C.S., Edin., and his correspondence with the Governor and the Executive Committee on the subject of his resignation and retirement from the Hospital. The Letter of L. Q. Bowerbank, Esq., F.R.C.P., & L.R.C.S., Edin., in reply to Dr. Fiddes & Dr. Fiddes reply to same; also the evidence adduced at the Coroners Inquest held on Richard Bailey, lately an inmate of the Public Hospital. *Kingston,* 1865

487a—REPORT ON LEPROSY by the Royal College of Physicians, preprepared for Her Majesty's Secretary of State for the Colonies; with an appendix. Abstracts of Replies to Interrogatories, prepared by the Leprosy Committee of the Royal College of Physicians. [later ed. of 486a.] *London,* 1867

488—THE REPORT of the Ordinary Medical Officers, and the Inspector of the Public Hospital, Kingston, Jamaica, for the year 1865. *Jamaica,* 1869

489—THE TERROR of the Tents, or Quarantine Restrictions as imposed and enforced in Jamaica, during the prevalence of small-pox, under so-called Paternal Government. [By Lewis Quier Bowerbank, M.D., F.R.C.P.]. *Jamaica,* 1872

490—THE MINERAL SPRINGS OF JAMAICA. By J. C. Phillippo, M.D. *Kingston,* 1881

The same. *Kingston,* 1891

491—TRUTH. Man's Noblest Defence. A refutation of charges made by the Editor of the "Gleaner" while writing on the subject of Fevers. By José Mayner. *Kingston,* 1881

492—CORRESPONDENCE relating to the Sanitary State of the Town of Port Royal. *Kingston,* 1883

493—ELECTRICITY as a Therapeutic Agent and its correlation to the vital principle or Nerve-Force. By José Mayner. *Kingston,* 1883

494—REPORT to the Board of Health of the state of Louisiana on the sanitary condition of the island of Jamaica. By Lucien F. Solomon, M.D. *New Orleans,* [1885]

495—CHOLERA in Jamaica in 1850, '51 and '54, and the Lessons to be learnt therefrom. A Lecture delivered at the request of the Sanitary Committee appointed by the Public Meeting held in Kingston in February, 1887. By Dr. J[ames] C[ecil] Phillippo, M.D., L.R.C.S. Ed. *Kingston.* [1887]

The same. Reprint. *Kingston,* 1892

496—CONTRIBUTION to the Medico-Military History of Jamaica, A "Retrospect" (an Expansion of a paper read before the Jamaica Branch of the British Medical Association, Kingston.) By S[amuel] E[dward] Maunsell, Brigade-Surgeon, Medical Staff. *Jamaica,* 1891

497—YELLOW FEVER IN THE WEST INDIES. By Izett Anderson, M.D., Edin. *London,* 1898

498—POPULAR LECTURE ON HYGIENE. Delivered before the Young Men's

Guild, Scotch Kirk, Kingston. By James Ogilvie, M.D., C.M. *Kingston,*   1900

499—RULES AND REGULATIONS of the New City Dispensary, Kingston, founded 3rd July, 1876, by the late B. A. Franklin. n.d.

VIII. AGRICULTURE AND HORTI-CULTURE.

500*A SHORT ACCOUNT of the interest and conduct of the Jamaica Planters, in an address to the Merchants, Traders and Liverymen of the City of London. *London,* 1754

501—*A TREATISE CONCERNING THE PROPERTIES AND EFFECTS OF COFFEE. By Benjamin Moseley 1775
The same. 3rd ed.   1785
The same. 5th ed.   1792

502—*AN ESSAY upon Pen-keeping and Plantership. By Patrick Klein [of St. Mary, Planter].   1797

503—*OBSERVATIONS AND ADVICES [on the manufacture of Sugar and Rum]. By Bryan Higgins, M.D. *St. Jago de la Vega,*   1797-1803.

504—REPORT FROM A COMMITTEE OF THE HONOURABLE HOUSE OF ASSEMBLY [OF JAMAICA] on the commerce and agriculture of the Island ; the probable effects thereon of opening the trade to the East Indies, and the operation of the present maximum on the exportation of sugar. *Jamaica,*   1813

505—EIGHT PRACTICAL TREATISES on the Cultivation of the Sugar Cane. Written in consequence of His Excellency the Earl of Elgin's offer of a prize of one hundred pounds in the latter part of 1842. [By Thomas Henny, Raynes W. Smith, W. F. Whitehouse, W. A. Clements, James Sullivan, G. W. Gordon and others], *Jamaica,*   1843

506—A TREATISE UPON THE MANUFACTURE OF SUGAR. Presented to the Royal Agricultural Society of Jamaica, June, 1844. By Veritas. Reprinted from the " Jamaica Times," 1844 ; also Observations on Recent Improvements, &c., by Henry Crosley. *London,*   1847

507—AGRICOLA'S LETTERS and Essays on Sugar Farming in Jamaica. By W. F. Whitehouse. *Kingston,*   1845

508—BYE-LAWS of Royal Agricultural Society of Jamaica, with the Act of Incorporation. *London,*   1845

509- * SUGGESTION FOR SEPARATING THE CULTURE OF SUGAR from the process of manufacture, with a plan for establishing a Central Sugar Factory at Annotto Bay, Jamaica. By Alexander Gordon Fyfe,   1846

510—* SMITH'S AGRICULTURAL SOCIETY FOR JAMAICA. Report of the Board of Directors to an extraordinay meeting of the proprietors convened for . . 20th . . . December, 1848, at Liverpool. *Manchester,*   1848

511—*GENERAL INSTRUCTIONS for Montpelier and Ellis Caymanas Estates in Jamaica. By H[oward] de W[alden]. June, 1852. Privately printed.   1852

512—SUGGESTIONS RELATIVE TO THE IMPROVEMENT OF THE BRITISH WEST INDIA COLONIES by means of instruction by Ministers of religion and schools. The Relations of Property and Labour, Agricultural and other industrial improvements, &c., with especial reference to the increased cultivation of the Sugar Cane and Cotton in Jamaica and British Guiana. By a resident in the West Indies for thirteen years [Mrs. Campbell, née Bourne]. With an introduction and concluding remarks by a late Stipendiary Magistrate in Jamaica [Stephen Bourne]. *London,*   1853

513—THE IMPORTANCE, NECESSITY AND PRACTICABILITY OF THOROUGH DRAINAGE IN THE BRITISH WEST INDIA COLONIES, in order to restore prosperity to those countries, as well as to render compulsory labour unnecessary to the production of an adequate supply of sugar and cotton. A letter to the Right Hon. the Earl of Aberdeen by a late Stipendiary Magistrate in Jamaica [Stephen Bourne]. *London,* 1853

514—TRANSACTIONS OF THE ROYAL SOCIETY OF ARTS. Vol. I. from Dec. 1854, to Dec. 1855 inclusive. Vol. II. from Jan. to Dec. 1856 inclusive. Vol. III. from Jan. to Dec. 1857 inclusive. Vol. IV. from July 1857 to April 1868. 4 vols. *Kingston,*   1854-1868

515—Rules of the Royal Society of Arts and Agriculture. *Kingston,* 1867

516—Annual Report of the Royal Society of Arts and Agriculture. 1867. *Kingston,* 1868

517—The Fall of the Sugar Planters of Jamaica, with remarks on their Agricultural Management and on the Labour Question in that Island. By Hall Pringle. *London,* 1869

518—Coffee. By D. Morris, M.A., F.G.S., *Kingston,* 1881

519—Root Food Growth in Jamaica. By Rev. Josias Cork. *Kingston,* 1881.

520—Stock and Stock-raising. By Archibald Roxburgh. *Kingston,* 1881

521—The Timbers of Jamaica. By W. Bancroft Espeut, F.L.S. *Kingston,* 1881

522—Cacao: how to grow and how to cure it. By D. Morris, M.A., F.L.S. *Kingston,* 1882

523—The Mongoose on Sugar Estates in the West Indies. By D. Morris, M.A., *Kingston,* 1882

524—The Cultivation of the Orange in Jamaica. By James Neish, M.D. *Kingston,* 1884

525—The Cultivation of Ramie. By J. C. Phillippo, M. D. *Kingston,* 1884

526—Native and other Fibre Plants. By D. Morris, M.A., F.L.S. *Kingston,* 1884

527—The Vine and its Culture. By the Rev. William Griffith. *Kingston,* 1884

528—Correspondence between the Government of Jamaica and Geo. Henderson, respecting the prices charged for Cinchona seeds, seedlings and plants, together with a few other particulars about Cinchona mortality and management in the Jamaica Government Nurseries. *Kingston,* 1884

529—Return of the several Sugar Estates and other Properties in Jamaica. *Kingston,* 1884

530—Lecture on the occurrence of Droughts, their causes and the means whereby their effects might be mitigated, modified or relieved . . . By D. Morris, M.A. *Kingston,* 1885

531—On a new Beverage Substance: the Kola Nut. By James Neish, M.D. *Kingston,* 1887

532—The most effective and practical means of ameliorating and extending the Agricultural and productive capabilities of Jamaica. . . . by Edward M. Earle. *Kingston,* 1887

533—Essay on the manufacture of Rum. By Samuel Stricker. *Kingston,* 1889

534—A Short Essay on the cultivation of the Sugar Cane suitable for Jamaica. By John Sundstrom. *Kingston,* 1890

The same. An Abbreviated Essay. . . . *Kingston,* 1890

535—Report of the Mongoose Commission, 1891. *Kingston,* 1891

536—Agricultural Show. Prize List, *Kingston,* 1891. 1891

537—An Agricultural Department for Jamaica: A discussion of the question at a meeting of the Jamaica Society of Agriculture and Commerce . . . on Monday, 6th June, 1892. *Jamaica,* 1892

538—Suggestions relative to the Advancement of Agriculture in Jamaica. By William H. Orrett. *Kingston,* 1892

539—Annuals and how to grow them. A Lecture. By William Cradwick. *Kingston,* 1892

540—The Jamaica Stud Book, with Historical Sketch of the Turf. Vol i. [all published]. By J. Thomson Palache. *Jamaica,* 1892

541—Kingston Horticultural Show. Prize Lists. *Kingston, Ja.,* 1892, 1893, 1894. 1896

542—Institute of Jamaica Lectures. Agriculture: By Wm. Fawcett, J. J. Bowrey, M. Grabham, J. T. Palache, B. S. Gosset, Adam Roxburgh, C. A. T. Fursdon, T. D. A. Cockerell and the Rev. Wm. Gillies. Treating of the Soil; Tillage and Manuring; Plant Life; Physiology of Farm Animals; the

Horse; Indian Cattle; Cattle in Jamaica; Dairying and Agricultural Pests; together with a classified list of books on Agriculture in the Library of the Institute. *Kingston,*
1893

543—REPORT OF THE SELECT COMMITTEE OF THE LEGISLATIVE COUNCIL ON AGRICULTURE, and

(ii.) Evidence taken by the Committee.

(iii.) Scheme to establish a Department of Agriculture in Jamaica, proposed by the Hon. T. H. Sharp. *Kingston,*
1895

544—THE LAND THE TRUE SOURCE OF JAMAICA'S PROSPERITY. A paper read by George Levy. *Kingston,*
1895

545—KINGSTON AND ST. ANDREW AGRICULTURAL SHOW 1896. Prize List and Catalogue of Stock. *Kingston,*
1896

546—REPORT on Cattle Disease in Jamaica. By Professor W. Williams, F.R.S.E., F.R.C.V.S. *Kingston,*
1896

547—JOURNAL OF THE JAMAICA AGRICULTURAL SOCIETY. 1897-1901. 5 vols. *Kingston,*   1897-1901

548—MANCHESTER AGRICULTURAL SHOW held at Kendal on 30th November, 1899. [Prize List and Catalogue.] *Kingston,*   1899

549—THE MONEAGUE AND PEDRO AGRICULTURAL SOCIETY. Prize List the second Agricultural Show will be held at Thickets, Saint Ann's on August 3rd, 1899. *St. Ann's Bay,*
1899

550—JAMAICA AGRICULTURAL SOCIETY'S SHOW will be held on the Race Course, Kingston, on 19th and 20th April, 1899. [Prize List.] *Kingston*   1899

551 MANCHESTER HORTICULTURAL SHOW to be held on 11th May, 1899, at the Mandeville Market. *Kingston,*
1899

552—ROYAL JAMAICA SOCIETY OF AGRICULTURE AND COMMERCE AND MERCHANT'S EXCHANGE. Fifteenth Annual Report of the Council for the year ending 31st May, 1899. *Kingston,*   1899

553—THE CONCISE AGRICULTURAL GUIDE: or Helps for small proprietors and cultivators. By an Experienced Agriculturalist. *Kingston,*   [1899]

554—PRIZE-LIST AND REGULATIONS OF AGRICULTURAL SHOW to be held on grounds south of the Mico College, Kingston, on 4th and 5th April, 1900, also Catalogue and Programme. *Kingston,*   1900

555—REPORT OF COMMITTEE respecting the establishment of an Agricultural Department and an Experiment Station. n. d. [*Kingston,*
1900].

556—THE ELTHAM PARK FARM, Spanish Town, Jamaica. 1901. Proprietor, Thos. H. Sharp. [Prospectus.] 1901

557—PORT ROYAL MOUNTAIN and Dallas Agricultural Show held at Hope Gardens on 1st and 2nd May, 1901. [Prize-List and Programme.]   [*Kingston* 1901]

558—A REPORT ON THE CULTIVATION OF PINE APPLES and other products of Florida. By Robert Thomson. (Jamaica Board of Agriculture). *Kingston,*   1901

IX. TRADE AND COMMERCE.

559—A LETTER FROM A MERCHANT AT JAMAICA to a Member of Parliament in London, touching the African Trade. . . . *London,*
1709

560—*THE FOLLOWING ADDRESS and particular instances as to the duties demanded on Prize goods brought into Jamaica were sent from that island by the Governor, Council and Assembly, in March 1709-10: whereupon an Act passed in the ninth year of Her Majesty's reign that prize goods should not be liable to the demand of duties by virtue of an Act entitled, an act to encourage to trade to America for the future: and all proceedings upon the bonds enter'd into were ordered to be staid until a clear state of those bonds could be had from Jamaica, and laid before this present Parliament. Since then an account of the said Bonds has been transmitted by the Governor, Council and Assembly of Jamaica to the Lords Commissioners of Trade and Plantations, &c. [*London*, ? 1712]

561—OCCASIONAL PAPERS ON THE ASSIENTO AND THE AFFAIRS OF JAMAICA [by William Wood] *London* 1716. (a) The Assiento Contract consider'd, as also the Advantages and Decay of the Trade of Jamaica and the Plantations, with the causes and consequences thereof. In several letters to a member of Parliament, 1714. (b) A True State of Mr. Aylmer's Brief Narrative. In a letter to —— London, 1716. (c) A View of the Proceedings of the Assemblies of Jamaica, for some years past, with some considerations on the Present State of that Island : in several occasional Papers, London 1716. (d) The Representation and Memorial of the Council of the Island of Jamaica to the Right Honourable the Lords Commissioners for Trade and Plantations. Together with the Addresses of the Governor and Council and Town of Kingston, and association of the principal inhabitants. With a preface by W. Wood. *London*, 1716

562—SOME OBSERVATIONS ON THE ASSIENTO TRADE, as it has been exercised by the South Sea Company ; proving the damage which will accrue thereby to the British commerce and plantations in America, and particularly to Jamaica. To which is annexed a sketch of the advantages of that Island to Great Britain, by its annual produce, and by its situation for trade or war. Addressed to His Grace the Duke of Newcastle, one of His Majesty's Principal Secretaries of State, by a person who resided several years at Jamaica. *London*, 1728

The same. 2nd ed. 1728

563—AN ANSWER TO A CALUMNY, with some Remarks upon an Anonimous Pamphlet address'd to His Grace the Duke of Newcastle, entitled : Some Observations on the Assiento Trade, as it has been exercised by the South Sea Company, &c., where by the damage which has or is likely to accrue thereby to the British

commerce and plantations, and particularly to Jamaica is also considered. By the Factor to the South Sea Company, at whom the calumny was aimed. *London*, 1728

564—A DEFENCE OF THE OBSERVATIONS ON THE ASSIENTO TRADE, as it hath been exercised by the South Sea Company, &c. In two parts. I. In relation to the Controversy. II. In relation to the Queries which were published in the Craftsman and other aspersions on the author of the Observations on the Assiento Trade, as well as on the Island of Jamaica. By the author of the Observations on the Assiento Trade. *London*, 1728

565—DESCRIPTION OF THE WINDWARD PASSAGE AND GULF OF FLORIDA, with the course of the British Trading ships to and from the Island of Jamaica. Also an account of the Trade-winds and of the variable winds and currents on the Coasts thereabouts, at different seasons of the year. Illustrated with a chart . . . whereby is demonstrated the precariousness of these voyages to the West India Merchants . . , 2nd ed. with additions. *London*, 1739

566—A HISTORY OF THE VOYAGES AND TRAVELS of Captain Nathaniel Uring. Very useful for Masters of ships that use the Leeward Island Trade, or Jamaica. *London*, 1749

567—*THE MERCHANTS, FACTORS AND AGENTS residing at Kingston in Jamaica, Complainants, against the inhabitants of Spanish Town, adjacent parishes, and against the Planters, Settlers and chief body of the people of the island of Jamaica Respondents. The Respondents' case. Privately printed. *London*, 1755

568—*AN INQUIRY CONCERNING THE TRADE, Commerce and Policy of Jamaica, relative to the scarcity of money . . to which is added a scheme for establishing a public bank. *St. Jago-de-la-Vega*, 1757

569—THE AMERICAN NEGOTIATOR : or the various Currencies of the British Colonies in America; as well the Islands, as the Continent. The Currencies of . . . Jamaica, reduced into English money. . . . By J. Wright. *London,* 1761

570—THE COMPLETE MERCHANT'S CLERK, or British American Counting-House. In two parts. . . . Part II. Contains book-keeping in factory, as at present used in the sundry factories of America, but in a more particular manner adapted to the Island of Jamaica . . . By William Weston. *London,* 1762

571— A LETTER TO THE MEMBERS OF GREAT BRITAIN, and the West-India Planters, recommending an increase on Freight of Sugars, &c., from Jamaica particularly, either by mutual consent, or law: a future prevention of such Rogues escaping justice as have heretofore done, by going to Jamaica, and other parts, with both ships and merchandize, and there remaining, in defiance of our present laws, to the detriment of the owners and creditors.. . . . *London,* 1769

572—THE WEST INDIA PILOT, containing Piloting directions for Port Royal and Kingston Harbours, in Jamaica, in and out through the Kays, &c., Morant Harbour, Morant Kays, Blewfields Bay, Manteca Bay, and Lucia Harbour . . . illustrated with maps and plans; engraved by the best artists. By Captain Joseph Smith Speer. *London,* 1771

573—*PROPOSAL FOR INTRODUCING INTO JAMAICA a quantity of gold and silver species sufficient to carry on the internal commerce of the Country without the assistance of any foreign Coin. By the Hon. F. Cooke. *St. Jago-de-la-Vega,* 1773

574—FREE AND CANDID REFLECTIONS occasioned by the late additional duties on Sugar and on Rum; submitted to the consideration of the British Ministry, the members of both Houses of Parliament and the proprietors of Sugar Estates in the West India Colonies. By John Gardner Kemeys (of Plantain Garden River Plantation in Jamaica). *London,* 1783

574a—*[RESOLUTIONS, PETITIONS AND MEMORIALS relative to the imports from different American Ports and their several returns, together with copies of the petitions from the different Parishes, and the Memorial to the Crown concerning the trade of Jamaica.] No title page. [Privately printed. *London,* 1785]

575—AN EXAMINATION into the true cause of the Stream which runs through the Gulf of Florida into the Atlantic Ocean: With directions for sailing from Jamaica through that Passage . . . By Lieut. James Manderson, R. N. *London,* 1804

576—AUTHENTIC PAPERS relating to the expediency of importing salted Beef, Pork, Butter and Fish into the Island of Jamaica, either freely from neutral and other States in amity with Great Britain, or exclusively from the British Dominions, in British vessels and by British subjects. Transmitted from Jamaica to the Chamber of Commerce of Dublin; *Dublin,* 1806

577—AN ESSAY ON TASK-WORK, its Practicability and the modes to be adopted for its application to different kinds of Agricultural Labour. *Jamaica.* n. d. [aft. 1809]

578—REMARKS ON THE PRESENT State of the Spanish Colonies, and the importance of Cuba to the interests of Great Britain in the Caribbean Sea. *Jamaica,* 1820

579—NARRATIVE of the Voyage from Montego Bay, in the Island of Jamaica, to England; by a route never gone before or since. . . . Performed in the Autumn, 1809. . . . By G. Hallam. *London,* 1831

580—THE ROYAL CHARTER for establishing a Colonial Bank. *Kingston,* 1836

581—THE CURRENCY [of Jamaica]. [? 1838]

582—COPY OF AN ACT passed by the Legislature of the island of Jamaica, in the month of December last, imposing duties on all articles imported into that island for internal consumption, together with copies or extracts of any correspondence relating thereto. Parliamentary Papers. *London,* 1843

583—COPY OF THE MEMORIAL to Her Majesty, of the House of Assembly of Jamaica, on the distressed condition of the colony. Parliamentary Papers. *London,* 1844

584—A TREATISE ON BOOK-KEEPING, composed by David Dias Fernandes. To form the minds of youth, and adapted to th · way the business is done in Jamaica. . . · *Kingston,* 1844

585—COPY OF THE MEMORIAL of the House of Assembly of Jamaica to Her Majesty, transmitted by the Governor on the 21st day of December last (re sugar and coffee). Parliamentary Papers. *London* 1845

586—BYE-LAWS of the Royal Agricultural Society of Jamaica with the Act of Incorporation. *London,* 1845

587—TERMS AND REGULATIONS for conducting cases submitted· for arbitration to the Jamaica Chamber of Commerce. *Kingston,* 1846

588·—REPORT TO THE JAMAICA CHAMBER OF COMMERCE, on the Duties Question in England, as the same might affect the future cultivation of the British West Indian Colonies. Presented to the Chamber by the Committee appointed to consider that subject, and other points connected with the Trade and Agriculture of Jamaica. *Kingston,* 1846

589—COPY OF MEMORIAL from the Chamber of Commerce of Kingston, Jamaica, to the Treasury; and of the report of the Chamber on the Sugar Duty Question. 1846

590—COPIES OR EXTRACTS of any correspondence between the Secretary of State for the Colonies and the Governor of Jamaica and Trinidad, respecting the operation of the Navigation Laws in those Islands. Parliamentary Papers. *London,* 1847

591—*REPORT OF THE STANDING COMMITTEE OF THE CHAMBER OF COMMERCE, Jamaica, upon the present condition of that Colony; the

causes of its depression; and the remedial measures necessary to restore its prosperity. *London,* 1847.

592—*RESOLUTIONS OF THE SEVERAL PARISHES in the counties of Surry, Middlesex, and Cornwall, and of the Chamber of Commerce, Jamaica; on the state of the Island consequent upon the admission of foreign Slave Sugar into the markets of Great Britain, etc. *Jamaica,* 1847

593—DESCRIPTIVE CATALOGUE of Articles exhibited by the Royal Society of Arts, Jamaica (assisted by the Society of Industry, Hanover, Jamaica) at the International Exhibition, 1862. By E[dward] C[hitty]. *London,* 1862

594—AN ESSAY on the Extension of Agricultural Credits in Jamaica. [By William Wemyss Anderson]. [*annotated by the author.*] *Kingston,* 1869

595—A DESCRIPTIVE CATALOGUE of the Collection sent from the Island of Jamaica to the Centennial Exhibition of 1876 at Philadelphia. Compiled . . by Robert Thomson. *Kingston,* 1876

596—INTERNATIONAL COLONIAL AND EXPORT TRADE EXHIBITION, Amsterdam, 1883. Catalogue of Articles illustrating the agricultural and industrial products of Jamaica, intended as a guide for the use of Exhibitors. *Kingston,* 1882

597—JAMAICA at the World's Exposition at New Orleans, 1884. *Kingston,* 1884

598—JAMAICA AT THE WORLD'S EXPOSITION [New Orleans]: an official introduction to the Jamaica Court, containing a short description of the island, its products and its climate. Kingston, 1884: also catalogue of articles forwarded from the island of Jamaica and on exhibition at the Jamaica Court, Main Building: prepared by D. Morris, M.A., F.L.S. *New Orleans,* 1885

599—RULES OF THE JAMAICA SOCIETY of Agriculture and Commerce. *Kingston,* 1885

600—JAMAICA AT THE COLONIAL and Indian Exhibition. London, 1886.

Catalogue of Articles forwarded from the island of Jamaica. *Kingston,*   1886

601—THE JAMAICA COURT at the Indian and Colonial Exhibition, 1886. Handbook compiled by Lawrence R. Fyfe, for the Governors of the Jamaica Institute. *Jamaica,* 1886

602—JAMAICA at the Colonial and Indian Exhibition. By C. Washington Eves, C.M.G. 4th ed. *London,* 1886

603—JAMAICA at the Colonial and Indian Exhibition, London, 1886. Executive Commissioner, in London; Sir Augustus J. Adderley, K.C.M.G, Royal Commissioner. Honorary Commissioner C. Washington Eves, Esq. [Illustrations, maps, and portraits.] [*London,* 1886]

—*The same.* 4th ed. *London,* 1886

604—JAMAICA at the Royal Jubilee Exhibition, Liverpool. 1887. By C. Washington Eves, C.M.G. *London,* 1887

605—JAMAICA INTERNATIONAL EXHIBITION, 1891. Preliminary Papers.
1890

606—JAMAICA EXHIBITION, Official Catalogues, Reports. List of Awards, Guides, &c. &c., of the Jamaica Exhibition of 1891. *Kingston,* 1891

607—A SHADE OF THE JAMAICA EXHIBITION, opened on the 27th January, 1891, in Kingston. By E. C. Hinchcliffe. *Kingston, Ja.,* 1891

608—JAMAICA EXHIBITION. Report of the Honorary Commissioner (Adam Brown) representing Canada at the Jamaica Exhibition. *Ottawa,* 1891

609—THE CULTIVATION OF THE OYSTER and its possible development around the coast of Jamaica. (From the "Gleaner" 1892).   1892

610—JAMAICA SOCIETY OF AGRICULTURE AND COMMERCE. Reports for 1886-1898, and Rules revised to 1896. *Kingston,*   1886-1898

The same. ROYAL JAMAICA SOCIETY OF AGRICULTURE and Com-

merce. Reports for 1899-1901. *Kingston,*   1899-1901

611—THE JAMAICA AND WEST INDIES FISHERIES: their position and Prospects. By Edward M. Earle. *London,* 1893

612—JAMAICA AT CHICAGO (World's Fair). An account descriptive of the Colony of Jamaica, with historical and other appendices. Compiled under the direction of Lt.-Col. the Hon. C. J. Ward, C.M.G., Honorary Commissioner for Jamaica. (Illustrated.) *New York,* 1893

613—JAMAICA FIBRE COMPANY. Prospectus, 1894

614—CARIBBEAN SEA FISHERIES DEVELOPMENT SYNDICATE, LIMITED. [Papers respecting.] 1894

615—OUR FISHERIES: To be or not to be. An Address to the people of Jamaica. By Edward M. Earle, J.P. *Kingston,* [1895]

616—PENKEEPERS ASSOCIATION. Prospectus. *Kingston,* 1896

617—MEMORANDUM AND ARTICLES OF ASSOCIATION of the Jamaica Fruit Transporting and Trading Company of London, Limited. Registered 31st July, 1896. *London,* 1896

618—THE DEVELOPMENT OF THE RESOURCES OF JAMAICA. By A. McDowell Nathan. *Kingston,* 1898

619—JAMAICA FISHERIES. The Operations in Jamaica of the Caribbean Sea Fisheries Development Syndicate. By J. E. Duerden, A.R.C.Sc. *Kingston,* 1898

620—TARIFF OF JAMAICA: effect upon Trade. (Advance Sheets of [United States] Consular Reports, July 19, 1899).   1899

621—PRIZE ESSAYS containing suggestions as to the opening up and development of trade between Bristol and Jamaica. [By (i.) Arthur L. Wilson, (2) W. Simpson McCormack]. *Liverpool,* 1900

622—BRISTOL CHAMBER OF COMMERCE AND SHIPPING. West India Trade Section. Souvenir of the Complimentary Banquet to His Excellency the Governor of Jamaica, Sir Augustus W. L. Hemming, G.C.M.G. *Bristol,* 1900

623—THE MARINE RESOURCES OF THE BRITISH WEST INDIES. By J. E. Duerden, Ph. D., A'.R.C.S. (Lond,) West Indian Bulletin. Extra Number. *Bridgetown, Barbados,* 1901

X. LAW AND POLITICS.

624—JOURNALS OF THE COUNCIL AND THE HOUSE OF ASSEMBLY. Commissions: Speeches by Governors: Accounts of the Island by various Governors: Other correspondence. 3 vols. ms. Vol. I. 1661-1688: Vol. II. 1687-1688: Vol. III. 1670-1692.

> [Note. Mss. transcribed from various sources, (e.g. Vol. II. is from the Sloane MS. 1599 in the British Museum in 1798) about 1798-1800 : apparently for the purposes of compiling " The Journals of the Assembly of Jamaica," published at Spanish Town in 1811—No. 657]. 1661-1692

625 —*A NARRATIVE OF AFFAIRS lately received from His Majestie's Island of Jamaica . . viz. : (i.) The Governor Sir T. Linch's speech to the Assembly . . . Sep- 21, 1682. (ii.) S. Bernard . . speaker of the said Assembly, his speech to the Governor. (iii.) An humble address from His Majestie's Council . . to . . his Majesty. (iv.) The Governor's Speech at the proroguing the Assembly. *London,* 1683

626—LAWS OF JAMAICA : passed by the Assembly and confirmed by His Majesty in Council, April 17th, 1684. To which is added the State of Jamaica, as it is now under the Government of Sir Thomas Lynch, with a large mapp of the Island. *London,* 1684

—*Bound with the above*: The Continuation of the Laws of Jamaica passed by the Assembly and confirmed by His Majesty in Council, December 26th, 1695: being the second volume of the said Laws. *London,* 1698

627—*AN ABRIDGEMENT of the Laws in force and use in Her Majesty's plantations, (viz.) of Virginia, Jamaica, Barbadoes, Maryland, New England, New York, Carolina, &c., digested under proper heads in the method of Mr. Wingate. *London,* 1704

628—*THE REPRESENTATION AND MEMORIAL of the Council of the Island of Jamaica to the Lords Commissioners for Trade and Plantations [complaining of the refusal of supplies, etc., by the General Assembly] together with the addresses of the Governour . . . . and Council, and Town of Kingston . . . With a preface by Mr. Wood. *London,* 1716

629—*A VIEW OF THE PROCEEDINGS of the Assemblies of Jamaica for some years past, with considerations on the present state of the Island : in several occasional papers. *London,* 1716

630—ACTS OF ASSEMBLY, passed in the Island of Jamaica from 1681 to 1737 inclusive. *London,* 1738

631—A LETTER TO A MEMBER OF PARLIAMENT concerning the Importance of our Sugar-Colonies to Great Britain. By a Gentleman who resided many years in the island of Jamaica. *London,* 1745

632—*A BILL for the better peopling of the island of Jamaica with white inhabitants : for encouraging the cultivation of lands at present uncultivated. [*Kingston ?* 1750 ?]

633—*A LETTER from a Citizen in Port Royal, Jamaica, to a Citizen of New York, relating to some extraordinary measures lately set on foot in that island. *Dublin* printed. *London* reprinted. n.d. [ab. 1756]

634—*AN HISTORICAL ACCOUNT of the Sessions of Assembly, for . . . Jamaica; which began on . . . the 23rd of Sept. 1755, being the Second Sessions of that Assembly. Containing a vindication of . . . C. Knowles . . . then Governor of that Island, &c. [MS- notes]. *London,* 1757

635—ACTS FOR OPENING and establishing certain Ports of the Islands of Jamaica and Dominica, for the more free Importation and Exportation of certain goods and merchandize . . . *London,* 1766

636—THE PRIVILEGES of the Island of Jamaica Vindicated; with an impartial narrative of the late Dispute between the Governor and House of Representatives upon the case of Mr. Olyphant, a member of that House. [With an Appendix. An Historical Account of the establishment of the Colony of Jamaica, drawn up by Sir William Beeston]. *Jamaica printed : London reprinted,* 1766

—*The same* a new ed., revised, corrected and considerably enlarged, to which is added A recent Case of Breach of Privilege. *Jamaica,* 1810

637—VOTES OF THE HONOURABLE THE HOUSE OF ASSEMBLY [for the years] 1784-85, 1790-94, 1796-1811, 1813-1866. 82 vols. *Jamaica,* 1785-1866

637a—*TWO REPORTS from the Committee of the Honourable House of Assembly of Jamaica. By Stephen Fuller. 1789

638—THE ACT OF ASSEMBLY of the Island of Jamaica to repeal several Acts, and clauses of Acts respecting Slaves, and for the better order and government of Slaves, and for other purposes; commonly called the Consolidated Act, as exhibiting at one view most of the essential Regulations of the Jamaica Code Noir; which was passed by the Assembly . . . 1787. *London,* 1788

639—THE NEW ACT of Assembly of the Island of Jamaica, intitled An Act to repeal an Act entitled An Act to repeal several Acts . . . , respecting Slaves . . . : and also . . . for consolidating and bringing into one Act the several Laws relating to Slaves . . . ; commonly called the new Consolidated Act . . . . passed 1788, being the present Code Noir of that Island. Published [with a preface] by S. Fuller, Agent for Jamaica. *London,* 1789

The same. An Act to repeal an Act, entitled, "An Act to repeal several acts and clauses of acts, respecting Slaves," etc. (6 Nov. 1788.) *St Jago de la Vega,* 1789

640—*AN ACT to repeal an Act, entitled, "An Act to prevent the enticing or inveigling of Slaves," &c., &c. (14th Oct., 1788.) *St. Jago de la Vega,* 1789

641—*AN ACT to oblige the several inhabitants of this Island to provide themselves with a sufficient number of white men, white women or white children, etc. (9 Dec. 1788.) *St. Jago de la Vega,* 1789

642—*AN ACT for repealing certain clauses of an act for repealing an act, entitled, "An Act for the better discovering and collecting the arrears of His Majesty's Quit-Rents," &c., (18 Dec. 1788.) *St. Jago de la Vega,* 1789

643—*AN ACT to explain and amend an act, entitled, "An Act for the more effectual prevention of smuggling," &c., (19 Dec. 1788.) *St. Jago de la Vega,* 1789

644—*AN ACT for laying a duty on all Wines, and upon Brandy, Gin, and other foreign Spirits, retailed within this Island, and on Rum sold for consumption, &c. (20th Dec., 1788.) *St. Jago de la Vega,* 1789

645—*AN ACT for raising a tax by the Poll, &c., (20th Dec. 1788.) *St. Jago de la Vega,* 1789

646—THE LAWS OF JAMAICA: comprehending all the Acts in force, passed between the thirty-second year of the reign of King Charles the Second, and the thirty-third year of the reign of King George the Third. To which is prefixed a Table of the Titles of the Public and Private Acts passed during that Time. Carefully revised and corrected from the original records; and published under the direction of Commissioners appointed for that purpose by 30 Geo. III. cap. XX and 32 Geo. III cap. XXIX. 2 vols. *St. Jago de la Vega,* 1792

647—PROCEEDINGS OF THE HON. HOUSE OF ASSEMBLY OF JAMAICA, on the Sugar and Slave-Trade, in a Session which began the 23rd of October, 1792. [*London*] 1793

648—AN ABRIDGMENT OF THE LAWS OF JAMAICA; being an Alphabetical Digest of all the Public Acts of Assembly now in Force from the thirty-second year of King Charles II. to the thirty-second year of his present Majesty King George III. inclusive, as published in two volumes under the direction of Commissioners appointed by 30 Geo. III. cap. XX. and 32 Geo. III. cap. XXIX, *St. Jago de la Vega*, 1793

The same. 2nd ed. *St. Jago de la Vega,* 1802

649—COMMITTEE OF CORRESPONDENCE. Letter Book, 1794-1833, Minute Book 1795-1846 (manuscript.) 2 vols. 1794-1846

650—AGENTS TO THE HON. COMMITTEE OF CORRESPONDENCE. Letters 1794-1801, 1814-1834. 4 vols. (manuscript.) 1794-1834

651—JOHN CAMPBELL, Appellant and William Beckford, Respondent ; and between John Swete and Henry Beke, Appellants and William Beckford, Respondent. Upon two separate appeals to His Majesty in Council, from an order made by the High Court of Chancery in the Island of Jamaica, dated the 0th of Sept., 1799. 1799

652—THE LAWS OF JAMAICA, Comprehending all the Acts in force, passed between the thirty-second year of the reign of King Charles the Second [1681] and the thirty-third year of the reign of King George the Third. 7 vols. *St. Jago de la Vega,* 1802-1824

653—THE LAWS OF JAMAICA : comprehending all the Acts in force, passed between the first year of the reign of King George the Third and the eleventh year of the reign of King George the Fourth inclusive. To which is prefixed a table of the titles of public and private acts passed during that time, carefully revised and corrected from the original records. second ed. 8 vols. [vol. 1 missing]. *St. Jago de la Vega,* 1802-1831

654—LAWS OF JAMAICA : 32 Chas. II. to 5 Victoria & 9 Victoria to 23 Victoria. 1st ed. 14 vols. *St. Jago de Vega & Kingston,* 1802-1856

655—OATHS taken and subscribed by Members of Assembly. (*Manuscript.*) [1803-1826]

856—WENTWORTH BAYLY, VS. REV. COLIN DONALDSON. Minutes of the proceedings of the trial of an action for defamation in the Grand Court, held in Spanish Town on Monday, 17th October, 1808. *Kingston,* 1808

657—JOURNALS OF THE ASSEMBLY OF JAMAICA. 1663-1826. Vol. 1-14 & index vol. 15 vols. *Jamaica,* 1811-1829

658—FURTHER PROCEEDINGS of the Honourable House of Assembly of Jamaica, relative to a Bill introduced into the House of Commons for effectually preventing the unlawful importation of slaves, and holding free persons in slavery in the British Colonies. To which are annexed examinations. taken upon oath before a Committee of that House for . . . disproving the allegations of the said Bill. *Jamaica,* 1816

659—*AN ACT in furtherance of the Provisions of the Abolition Laws within this Island. [dated 19th Dec., 1816] *Jamaica,* 1817

660—*AN ACT in aid of the several Acts relating to Aliens and persons of suspected character arriving in this Island. [dated 19th Dec., 1816]. *Jamaica* 1817

661—*AN ACT in aid of the Militia Law, &c., [dated 19th Dec., 1816]. *Jamaica,* 1817

662—*An ACT for raising a Tax by the Poll and on trades, supercargoes, &c. [dated 19th Dec., 1816]. *Jamaica,* 1817

663—*AN ACT for a more particular Return of Slaves in this Island and the enrolment thereof. [dated 11 Dec., 1816]. *Jamaica,* 1817

664—AN ACT for raising a Tax on Land within this Island, and applying the same to the public service. [dated 20 Nov., 1816.] *Jamaica,* 1817

665—*AN ACT for making further and other provision for collecting the public Taxes. [dated 20 Nov., 1816]. *Jamaica,* 1817

666—*AN ACT for laying a duty upon all wines and upon Brandy, Gin, Rum, &c. [dated 20 Nov., 1816]. *Jamaica,* 1817

667—AN ABSTRACT of the Laws of Jamaica relating to Slaves (from 33

Charles II. to 59 George III. inclusive) with the Slave Law at length : also an appendix containing an abstract of the Acts of Parliament relating to the abolition of the Slave Trade. By John Lunan. *St. Jago de la Vega,*　1819

668—REPORT of the Debate in the House of Commons, June 16th, 1825 on Dr. Lushington's motion respecting the deportation of Messrs. L. C. Lecesne, and J. Escoffery, two persons of colour from Jamaica. (From Hansard's Parliamentary Debates. New Series, vol. xiii., p. 1173.) *London,* n. d. [?1825]

669—ST. GEORGE'S. Slave Trials.
1822-1831

670—*THE NEW SLAVE LAWS of Jamaica . . Examined with . . reference to the eulogies pronounced upon them in Parliament. Society for the . . abolition of Slavery. *London,*　1828

671—THE CONSOLIDATED SLAVE LAW, passed the 22nd December, 1826, commencing on the 1st May, 1827, with a commentary (shewing the difference between the new law and the repealed enactments), marginal notes, and a copious index. 2nd ed. Carefully compared with the original. [*Kingston*],　1827

672—*EXPOSITION OF LAWS, &c., in Jamaica. By Clement. *Kingston,*
1828

673—*ADDRESSES and Memorials to His Majesty from the House of Assembly at Jamaica. Voted in the years 1821 to 1826 inclusive, and which have been presented to His Majesty by the Island Agent. Presented by the order of the House of Assembly of Jamaica. [*London,*
1828]

The same. 2nd ed. *London,* 1828

674—SLAVE LAW OF JAMAICA. With Proceedings and Documents relative thereto. *London,*　1828

675—MAGISTRATE'S AND VESTRYMAN'S ASSISTANT, containing a Digest of all the Laws of the Island, alphabetically arranged, from 33 Charles II. to 8 George IV., with forms of holding Quarter-Sessions, Coorner's Inquests, oaths, warrants, summonses recognizances, &c. [By

John Lunan, jr., Barrister-at-law). *St. Jago . e la Vega,*　1828
The same. 2nd ed. [to 5 William IV.] *St. Jago de la Vega,*　1835

678—A LETTER to the Rt. Hon. Sir George Murray, G.C.B., His Majesty's Principal Secretary of State for the Colonies, relative to the deportation of Lecesne and Escoffery from Jamaica. [By W. Burge]. *London,*　1829

677—LEWIS CELESTE LECESNE AND JOHN ESCOFFERY :—
Part I. Papers relating to the case of Lewis Celeste Lecesne and John Escoffery ; with Appendix.
Part II. Report of the Debate in the House of Commons, June 16th, 1825, on Dr. Lushington's motion respecting the Deportation of Messrs. L. C. Lecesne and J. Escoffery, . . . *London.*
Part III. Extracts from Mr. Burge's Printed Letter to the Right Honourable Sir George Murray : and observations thereon. Intended as a short Exposition of the Proceedings of the Government and the Supreme Court of Jamaica, in the case of Lecesne and Escoffery. *London,*　1830
Part IV. Report of the Trial of Mr. John Murray in the Court of King's Bench at Westminster Hall, the 19th December, 1829, on an Indictment for a Libel on Messrs. Lecesne and Escoffery of Jamaica. *London,*　1830

678—THE JAMAICA PETITION for representation in the British House of Commons, or for Independence. By Augustin H[ardin] Beaumont, a member of the Jamaica Assembly. [*London*].　1831

679—COPY OF A LETTER addressed to a Member of the Legislative Assembly of Jamaica by one of its members now in England [Anthony Davis]. *London,*　1832

680—*THE CASE OF WILLIAM RAMSAY, Inspector-General of Police, Jamaica, on a charge preferred against him by the Hon. Thomas James Bernard for a supposed obstruction of the law in reference to an alleged riot at a public meeting held at Spanish Town, 16 April, 1836. *London,*　1836

681—ACCOUNTS of slave compensation claims, for the Colonies of Jamaica, Caymanas . . . Parliamentary Papers. *London,* 1838

682—THE SPEECH of Mr. Sergeant Merewether at the Bar of the House of Commons, against the Bill intituled "An Act to make temporary provision for the government of Jamaica," Tuesday 23rd April, 1839. *London,* 1839

683- A LETTER TO THE COLONIAL SECRETARY on the precarious tenure of the Island of Jamaica and other West Indian Possessions. By an Anglo-Indian. *London,* 1839

684—A LETTER to the Marquess of Normanby relative to the present state of Jamaica, and the measures which are rendered necessary by the refusal of the House of Assembly to transact business. By Peter Howe, 2nd Marquess of Sligo. *London,* 1839

685—LETTER to the Viscount St. Vincent on the Jamaica House of Assembly's abandonment of its Legislative Functions. By Chas. Edward Long, Esq. *London,* 1839

686—REASONS for temporarily suspending the Constitution of Jamaica. *London,* 1839

687—PAPERS RELATIVE TO THE WEST INDIES. Part I. Circular Instructions. Jamaica. . . [*London*] 1839

688—THE JAMAICA QUESTION : Papers relative to the condition of the Labouring Population of the West Indies. Presented to Parliament by Her Majesty's command, 1839. By permission. *Lindfield,* 1839

689—SPEECH OF HIS EXCELLENCY the Right Hon. Sir C. T. Metcalfe, Bart., G.C.B., Governor of Jamaica, on proroguing the Jamaica Legislature on the 11th April, 1840. *London,* 1840

690—THE SPEECH OF . . . SIR C. T. METCALFE . . . on opening the Jamaica Legislature on the 27th of October, 1840, and the addresses of the Council and the Assembly in answer thereto, etc. 1840

691- PARLIAMENTARY PAPERS relative to the affairs of Jamaica. *London,* 1841

692—COPY of the Memorial of the Council and Assembly of Jamaica to Her Majesty against the reduction of the duties on foreign sugar. Parliamentary Papers. 1841

693—ABSTRACTS of the net revenue raised in the Island of Jamaica in the years 1838-39; of the expenditure or appropriation of the same, and of the number of slaves according to the last registration in 1832. Parliamentary Papers. 1841

694—REPORT of the Commissioners appointed under the 3rd Victoria, chapter 62, to ascertain and report what Laws of this Island it would be expedient to repeal, amend and consolidate. *Spanish Town,* 1842

695—THE REVISED STATUTES OF JAMAICA as to Crimes and Misdemeanours : analytically and alphabetically arranged, down to the Session 6th of Victoria, Anno 1842-43 inclusive. *London,* 1844

696—THE CONSTITUTION OF JAMAICA : Political, Judieial, and Ecclesiastical, including the Annual Laws of that Colony in force for 1844. *London,* 1844

The same. THE POLITICAL CONSTITUTION OF JAMAICA, including the Judicial and Ecclesiastical Establishments of that Colony and its Annual Laws in force for 1844. *London,* 1844

697—THE LAWS OF JAMAICA relating to the Administration of Civil Justice and to private persons and property (alphabetically and analytically arranged) down to the Session 9th of Victoria. 1845-46. *Kingston,* 1846

698—A LETTER ADDRESSED TO THE PUBLIC OF JAMAICA ; on the Political and Financial state of the Colony. By George Scotland, Esq., late member of the Honourable House of Assembly, for the Parish of Metcalfe. *Kingston,* 1847

699—A DIGEST of the Public Acts of the Island of Jamaica, including such statutes of England and of the United Kingdom of Great Britain and Ireland as are reputed and deemed in force in that Island

down to the year 1848, inclusive, analytically and alphabetically ar ranged. Vol. 1.   4to.; *Jamaica,*
1848

700—-MOTION PAPERS of the House of Assembly. 3 vols. *Jamaica,*
1849-1852

701—PAPERS relative to the Affairs of the Island of Jamaica. Presented to both Houses of Parliament by command of Her Majesty, 10th May. *London,*   1849

702— PAPERS relative to the Legislative Proceedings in Jamaica. [Retrenchment, vol. 4.] Presented to both Houses of Parliament by command of Her Majesty, June 30, 1853.   Papers relative to the affairs of the island of Jamaica presented to both Houses of Parliament Aug. 10, 1854. *London,*   1853-1854

703—JOURNALS of the Honourable the Legislative Council of Jamaica, 1854-1866. 12 vols. *Kingston,*
1855-1866

704—*THE COURTS OF JAMAICA AND THE JURISDICTION. By an Island Solicitor. pt. 1. *London,*   1855

705—-DEBATES OF THE HONOURABLE HOUSE OF ASSEMBLY of Jamaica. Commencing from the third session of the first General Assembly under the New Constitution. Compiled by Abraham Judah and A[ugustus] C[onstantine] Sinclair, [1856-1866] 14 vols. [vols 2–14 are entitled Parliamentary Debates.] *Spanish Town,*   1857–1866

706—A DIGEST OF THE LAWS OF JAMAICA, from 33 Charles II. to 28 Victoria. By James Minot. [*Kingston,*]   1865
[See also 714 and 716]

707—COPY OR EXTRACTS of all Correspondence between the Secretary of State for the Colonies and the late Governor and late Lieut.-Governor of Jamaica respecting the establishment of Party Government or Responsible Government in that island. Also Copy of a Report presented to the House of Assembly of Jamaica by a Committee appointed to consider and report to the House on certain points connected with the proposed Tramway between Spanish Town and Porus. [*London,*]   1865

708—*JAMAICA : WHO IS TO BLAME? Reprinted from two articles in the 'Eclectic Review' entitled " The Problem" and " Jeopardy of Jamaica." By a Thirty Years' Resident. With an illustration and notes by the Editor of the 'Eclectic Review' [E. P. Hood]. *London,*
1866

709—*A QUARTER CENTURY OF JAMAICA LEGISLATURE. By J. M. Ludlow. *London,*   1860

710—MINUTES OF THE LEGISLATIVE COUNCIL OF JAMAICA. 1866-1902 43 vols. [vols. 1-3 and 31 missing]. *Kingston,*   1866-1902

711—-COMMENTARIES UPON MARTIAL LAW, with special reference to its regulation and restraint ; with an Introduction, containing Comments upon the Charge of the Lord Chief Justice in the Jamaica Case. By W. F. Finlason. *London,*   1867

712—THE STATUTES AND LAWS OF JAMAICA from Chafles II. 1680,, to Victoria, 1887. [The first 4 vols., from. 1680-1866., revised ed.] 9 vols. *Kingston,*   1867-1887
[For continuation see No. 743.]

713—A HISTORY OF THE JAMAICA CASE founded upon official or authentic Documents, and containing an account of the Debates in Parliament and the criminal prosecutions arising out of the case. By W. F. Finlason. *London,* [1868]
[For 2nd ed. see No. 92.]

714—CONTINUATION SUPPLEMENT TO THE DIGEST OF THE LAWS OF JAMAICA ; 31 and 32 Victoria, 1868. By James Minot. [See No. 706.] With Chronological Table of Acts [expired . . . repealed and in force] and Index by William Rastrick Lee. *Jamaica,*   1869

715—REPORT OF THE TRIAL OF THE ACTION OF TRESPASS against Sir John Peter Grant, K.C.B., Governor of Jamaica, and others, in the case of the schooner *La Have,* before the Hon. Sir John Lucie-Smith, Knt., C.M.G., Chief Justice.   By Henry Frederick Figueroa, Reporter. *Kingston,* [1870]

716—A SUPPLEMENT TO THE DIGEST OF THE LAWS OF JAMAICA, containing those passed in the year 1869, 32 and 33 Victoria. (With chronological Table of Acts and Laws expired, repealed and in force . . . .) By William Rastrick Lee. *Jamaica,* 1870

The same for the year 1870, 33 and 34 Victoria. [With chronological table of Acts and Laws, expired . . . repealed and in force . . . .] *Jamaica,* 1871

The same for the years 1871-72. 35 and 36 Victoria. *Kingston,* 1874

717—GENERAL RULES AND FORMS of the Jamaica District Courts, under the Bankruptcy Law, 1871 . . . *Jamaica,* 1872

718—CORRESPONDENCE regarding the alleged keeping of private Lock-Ups by Magistrates in Jamaica. *London,* 1872

719—*JAMAICA LAW REPORTS, published by direction of the Governor, under the authority of the Judges of the Supreme Court. *Kingston,* 1873-78

720—ESTIMATES as passed by the Legislative Council for 1875-76 to 1902-3, 27 vols. *Kingston,* 1875-1902

721—JAMAICA. A Letter addressed to the Editor of the " Times." [By A. Lindo. 1877]

722—INDEX to the Laws of Jamaica, to 31st December, 1879. By W. A. Feurtado, [With chronological tables of Laws in force and repealed since the publication of the revised Statutes to 31st December, 1879, and Appendix.] *Kingston,* 1880

The same. To 31st December. 1888. *Kingston,* 1889

The same. 1892. *Kingston.* 1892

723—COPY OR EXTRACTS OF CORRESPONDENCE relating to a Memorial or Memorials received from Jamaica setting forth the grievances which have arisen under the system of Crown Government in that island, with the prayer or prayers of such memorials, and the number of signatures attached thereto. Parliamentary Paper. *London,* 1881

724—A FEW AMONG MANY FACTS concerning Crown Government in Ja-

maica and how it is administered. *Kingston,* 1881

725—IMPERIAL LAWS AND INSTRUCTIONS AS TO FOREIGN ENLISTMENT, EXTRADITION AND FUGITIVE OFFENDERS. Printed for the Government. *Kingston,* 1882

726—CORRESPONDENCE respecting the case of the ship " Florence." Presented to Parliament. *London,* 1882

727—SPEECHES DELIVERED BY A. LINDO, at a public meeting held in Falmouth on 17th Oct., 1882, and a Letter addressed by him to the Editor of the Trelawny and Public Advertiser, on the demand made upon the Colony for payment of the damages and costs in the actions to which the detention of the Florence gave rise, and on the recent appointments to the seats in the Council rendered vacant by the resignation of Messrs. S. C. Burke and J. C. Macglashan. [*Falmouth,* ?1882]

728—JAMAICA CIVIL SERVICE COMMISSION REPORT. *Kingston,* 1882

729—LETTER FROM GEORGE HENDERSON to Colonel Crossman, R.E., and George Baden-Powell, Esq., Royal Commissioners. *Kingston,* 1883

730—MEMORANDA on Certain points of inquiry concerning the Finances of the Island of Jamaica. *Kingston,* 1883

731—JAMAICA CONSTITUTION. ORDER IN COUNCIL. [1884]

732—REPORT of the Royal Commission appointed in December, 1882, to inquire into Public Revenues, Expenditure, Debts and Liabilities of the Island of Jamaica . . To which is added a Supplement to the Jamaica Gazette, containing a report by Colonel Crossman, C.M.G., R.E., and George Baden-Powell, M.A.. on the West Indian Incumbered Estates Court. Also further correspondence respecting the West Indian Incumbered Estates Court. *London,* 1884.

733—AN INDEX to the Acts and Laws of Jamaica, up to the close of the Session of 1883 : to which are added two Tables ; the one showing the

English Acts which have been adopted by the Legislature of Jamaica, the other, the Acts and Laws of Jamaica which are founded on English Acts. By Henry H. Hocking. *Kingston*   1884

734—FORM OF GOVERNMENT IN JAMAICA. Speech by Captain Price. House of Commons, April 25th, 1884. *London,*   [1884]

735—DEBATE on the Notice of motion of Captain G. E. Price, M.P., respecting the Government of Jamaica. Delivered in the House of Commons, April 25th, 1884. . . *London,*   1884

736—JAMAICA. Papers relating to proposed change in the form of government. [With a preface by Captain George E. Price, M.P.] *London,*   1884

737—PETITION from the inhabitants of Jamaica for a change in the Constitution of that Colony; together with the reply of Her Majesty's Government thereto, and accompanying correspondence. Presented to Parliament. *London,*   1884

738—FURTHER CORRESPONDENCE respecting the Constitution of the Legislative Council. Presented to Parliament. *London,*   1884

739—CORRESPONDENCE on Confederation with the Dominion of Canada. By Charles Levy. *Kingston,*   1885

740—AN INDEX TO THE RESIDENT MAGISTRATES' LAW, No. 43 of 1887, and the Laws in amendment thereof—Nos. 9 of 1888, 34 of 1888, and 10 of 1889. To which are added the Schedules of Court and other Fees. By Lionel L. Samuel. *Kingston,*   1889

741—THE STATUTES AND LAWS of the Island of Jamaica: Revised edition by the Hon. C. Ribton Curran, Acting Chief Justice of Jamaica. Charles II. to Law 40 of 1888. 12 vols. *Jamaica,*   1889

742—HANDBOOK OF THE LEGISLATIVE COUNCIL OF JAMAICA, including its constitution and the instructions regulating the same, and the Standing Rules and Orders thereof. *Jamaica,*   1889

743—THE LAWS OF JAMAICA. [1 of 1888 to 25 of 1901]. 16 vols. *Kingston,*   1888-1901

744—PROCEEDINGS OF THE LEGISLATIVE COUNCIL OF JAMAICA. 1891-1899. 9 vols. *Kingston,*   1892-1899

745—CORRESPONDENCE respecting Change in the Constitution of the Legislative Council of Jamaica. (Presented to both Houses of Parliament by command of Her Majesty, April, 1893). *London,*   1893

746—AN INDEX to the Acts and Laws of Jamaica up to Law No. 1 of 1892; compiled by W. Brandford Griffith, Resident Magistrate for the Parish of St. Elizabeth. *Jamaica,*   1892

The same. With an appendix (Civil Procedure Code). Compiled by Sir W[illiam] Brandford Griffith, Chief Justice of the Gold Coast, late Resident Magistrate for the parish of St. Elizabeth. 2nd ed. With three appendices, Resident Magistrates Law, Bill of Exchange Code and Bankruptcy Law by Charles M. Calder, Resident Magistrate for the parishes of Westmoreland and Hanover. *Jamaica,*   1900

747—THE ELEMENTARY EDUCATION LAW, 1892-94. [*Kingston,*]   1894

748—PRELIMINARY REPORT OF THE COMMITTEE appointed by His Excellency the Governor to make further reductions in the expenditure of the colony of Jamaica, and a report of the minority of the members of this Committee, July, 1898. *Kingston,*   1898

749—FURTHER CORRESPONDENCE relating to the Finances and Government of the island of Jamaica, presented to Parliament, July, 1899. *London,*   1899

750—COMMISSION OF ENQUIRY into the working of Parochial Boards appointed by H. E. the Governor, 4th February, 1899. Report by S. Leslie Thornton, Esq., on nine parishes. [*Jamaica,*   1899]

751—CORRESPONDENCE relating to the Public Finance and Revenues of the island of Jamaica. Presented to both Houses of Parliament. February, 1899. *London,*   1899

752—REPORT ON THE FINANCES OF JA-
MAICA by Sir David Barbour, pre.
sented to Parliament, July, 1899
London, 1899
The same. Kingston, 1899

753—DIGEST OF REVENUE LAWS AND
DEPARTMENTAL ORDERS, &c., compiled by Edward A. Savage, Col-
lector of Taxes, Trelawny. *Kingston,* 1900

754—FURTHER CORRESPONDENCE relating to the Finances and Government of the Island of Jamaica.
Presented to both Houses of Parliament, April, 1900. *London,* 1900

XI. EDUCATION.

755—SCHOOLS AND EDUCATION, JA-
MAICA. Copy of an Abstract of
Returns made by the Receiver-Ge-
neral and Clerks of Vestries. *London,* 1837

756—REPORT FROM C. J. LATROBE on
Negro Education in Jamaica : with
Correspondence relating thereto.
(Parliamentary Report). *London,*
1838

757—REPORT of the Trustees of Lady
Mico's Charity. *London,* 1838

758—SIX ESSAYS ON THE BEST MODE OF
ESTABLISHING AND CONDUCTING IN-
DUSTRIAL SCHOOLS, adapted to the
wants and circumstances of an agri-
cultural population. Written for
a prize of one hundred pounds of-
fered by His Excellency the Earl
of Elgin, Governor of Jamaica, in
November, 1843. I, by Lyndon
Howard Evelyn : II, by John Bu-
chanan ; III, by Rev. Josiah Cork ;
IV, by Rev. C. Stewart Renshaw ;
V, " Anonymous" ; VI, by Henry
Vendryes. *London,* 1845

759—NEW MODE OF CONDUCTING AGRI-
CULTURAL SCHOOLS on the outlines
of an Infant Agricultural Training
School, proposed for and dedicated
to the Royal Agricultural Society
of Jamaica. By Alex. Macleod.
Kingston, 1846

760—A CATECHISM of the History of
Jamaica : to which is added a Geographical and Topographical Catechism of that island, compiled from
the best authorities, for the use of
Schools. By Philip C. Labatt.
Kingston, 1848

761—A CONCISE CATECHISM of the Geography, History, Soil, Climate, &c.,
of the Island of Jamaica and its Dependencies. Compiled from the best
Authorities, for the use of Schools.
By Charles Plummer. *Kingston,*
1862

762—JAMAICA. A Manual of Geography, compiled for the use of beginners. By Thomas C. Moore,
A.S.M., 3rd W.I.R. *Kingston,*
1866

763 —THE ETYMOLOGY OF JAMAICA
GRAMMAR. By a Young Gentleman [Thomas Russell]. *Kingston,*
1868

764—JAMAICA : Outlines of its geography and history compiled expressly for the use of Schools : to
which is added a chapter comprising general information with regard
to the island. By Laurence R. Fyfe
and A. C. Sinclair. *Kingston,* 1883
The same. 5th ed. corrected and
revised. *Kingston,* 1890

765—POTSDAM SCHOOL. Calendar,
Christmas 1883, and 1886. *K ng-
ston,* 1884, and 1886

766—SUPPLEMENT TO SIR J. D. HOOK-
ER'S BOTANY PRIMER for use in
Jamaica Schools and Training Col-
leges. Prepared by J. H. Hart.
Kingston, 1887

767—LADY MICO'S CHARITY. General
Rules for the guidance of the Board
of Directors, Officers and Students
of the Mico Institution. Kingston,
February, 1887. *Kingston,* 1889

768—CODE OF REGULATIONS OF THE
EDUCATION DEPARTMENT, Jamaica,
approved by the Governor. *King-
ston,* 1890
The same : in force from 10th Au-
gust, 1893 under the provisions
of the Elementary Education Law,
1892. [*Kingston,*] 1893
The same : in force from 21st
March, 1895. *Jamaica,* 1895
The same : in force from 10th
May, 1900. *Kingston,* 1900
The same : in force from 1902.
[*Kingston*] 1902

769—ELEMENTARY CLASS BOOK of the
Geography and History of Jamaica.
By [Rev.] William Simms, M.A.
Kingston, 1891

769a—An Elementary text-book of Tropical Agriculture. By H. A. Alford Nicholls, M.D., F.L.S., illustrated. *Jamaica,* 1891

 The same. 2nd ed. Text-book of Tropical Agriculture. *London and New York,* 1902

769b—Examination Papers, Training Colleges. *Cambridge,* 1893-1901

769c—Examination Papers. Pupil Teachers Examinations. *Cambridge,* 1893-1902

770—Scheme in aid of Wolmer's Free School, and Report on condition of Funds of Trust. Kingston, 1894. By-Laws for the management of Wolmer's Free School. [*Kingston,* 1894]

 The same. By-Laws. [*Kingston,* 1900]

771—Bulletin of the Education Department, Jamaica. Published under the authority of the Superintending Inspector of Schools. Twelve numbers. *Kingston,* 1895-1898

772—Jamaica Union of Teachers. Rules of the n. d.

 The same. Report for 1897. 1897

773—A Catechism of the Discoveries of the West Indies and of North America, compiled expressly for Schools in Jamaica. By Samuel Jarrett. *Kingston,* 1897

774—Report of the Commission appointed to enquire into the system of Education in Jamaica, 1898, with Evidence and Appendix. *Kingston,* 1898

775—Gage's Practical System of Vertical Writing. Jamaica ed. n. d.

776—The Jamaica High School. Calendar. Christmas, 1899. *Kingston,* 1900

777—Special Reports on the System of Education in the West Indies and in British Guiana. (Sectional Reprint—Board of Education). [Jamaica. Part I by the Hon. Thomas Capper. Part II by M. E. Sadler]. *London,* 1901

778—Notes, Suggestions and Experiments for teaching the Science prescribed in the Code of Education for Elementary Schools. [By R. B. Strickland, B.A., and W. R. Buttenshaw, M.A. *Kingston,* 1901]

779—Shortwood College. Report of the Directors, 1901. [*Kingston,* 1901]

780—Report of a Discussion at a meeting of the Board of Education held October 23rd and 24th, 1900, on the method of paying grants-in-aid to Elementary Schools. *Kingston,* 1901

781—Statement by the Jamaica Schools Commission relating to the Jamaica High School and University College, 1901. [*Kingston,* 1901]

782—Outlines of the Geography and History of Jamaica. An elementary class book for schools. By A. Bruce McFarlane. *Toronto,* [1902]

XII. Sermons.

783—A Sermon preached at the funeral of His Excellency Sir Basil Keith, Knt., Governor of Jamaica, in the parish church of St. Catherine, and town of St. Jago de la Vega, June 16, 1777. By John Lindsay, D.D., Rector of that metropolis. *London,* 1780

784—The Inseparability of External Baptism and Internal Regeneration (in every case, both adult and infant) weighed in the balances of Experience, Scripture and the formularies of the Church of England, and found wanting. By the Rev. John Magrath . . . Minister of St. Michael's Church. *Spanish Town,* 1844

785—A Charge delivered at the primary visitation of The Clergy of the Archdeaconry of Jamaica in the Cathedral Church of St. Jago de la Vega, 12th Dec., 1844. By Aubrey George [Spencer], Lord Bishop of Jamaica. *Spanish-Town,* 1845

786—Correspondence relating to a sermon preached in the Cathedral-church St. Jago de la Vega on the evening before Good Friday, April 8th, 1852. *Kingston,* 1852

787—Lord Palmerston's Letter to the Presbytery of Edinburgh examined. A Sermon preached in the

Scotch Church, April 2nd, 1854, by the Revd. J[ohn] Radcliffe. With an appendix containing notes and the letter of Lord Palmerston. *Kingston,* [1854]

788—A PRIMARY CHARGE, delivered at the convocation of the Clergy of Jamaica, holden in Spanish-Town on the 15th April, 1858, by Reginald Courtenay, D.D., Bishop of Kingston. *Kingston,* [1858]

789—*THE OPERATIONS OF THE SPIRIT. A Sermon preached in the Parish Church of Kingston in reference to the Religious Revivals in this Island, on Sunday, the 6th of January, 1861, by Reginald Courtenay, D.D., Bishop of Kingston. *Kingston,* 1861

790—THE CHURCH HERSELF THE SOURCE OF HER REVENUES. By Rev. William Gillies. *Glasgow,* 1865

791—THREE PASTORAL CHARGES : addressed to the Clergy of the Diocese of Jamaica, in the years 1858, 1862 and 1868. By Reginald Courtenay, D.D., Bishop of Kingston. *Kingston,* [1868]

791a—THE OLD YEAR AND THE NEW : two Sermons by C. F. Gray, priest of the Church of England. *Kingston,* 1869

792—A PASTORAL CHARGE, addressed to the Clergy and Laity of the Diocese of Jamaica, in the year 1873. By Reginald Courtenay, D.D., Bishop of Kingston. *Kingston,* 1873

793—A SERMON on the death of W. Wemyss Anderson, delivered July 21, 1877 in the Scotch Kirk, Kingston, Jamaica, by the Rev. John Radcliffe. *Kingston,* 1877

794—THE JESUS OF HISTORY AND THE JESUS OF TRADITION IDENTIFIED, by George Solomon. A Review by the Rev. J[ohn] Radcliffe. *Kingston,* 1880

795—GLIMPSES OF THE EVIDENCE FOR THE MESSIAHSHIP OF JESUS OF NAZARETH, in connection with Notes and Strictures on a recent Anti-Christian work, entitled " The Jesus of History and the Jesus of Tradition identified." By the Rev. D. R. Morris, in eight parts. 3 vols. *Kingston,* 1881, 1882

796—A SERMON preached by Rev. H. M. F. MacDermot, Rector of St. Mark's Craigton at a Conference of Clergy and Laity, held in Spanish-Town, Aug. 12th, 1887. *Kingston,* 1887

797—A CHARGE delivered to the Clergy and Lay Representatives of the Diocese of Jamaica in Synod assembled 8th February, 1888. By the Right Revd. E. Nuttall, D.D., Bishop of Jamaica. *Kingston,* 1888

798—SERMONS for the use of Catechists and Lay Readers, Diocese of Jamaica. [Edited by Enos Nuttall, D.D., Bishop of Jamaica]. *Kingston,* 1890

799—THE IMPORTANCE AND POSSIBILITY OF ATTAINING RELIABLE RELIGIOUS KNOWLEDGE An address to men delivered by the Bishop of Jamaica [E. Nuttall], 8th April, 1892. *Kingston,* 1892

800—LETTER to professing Christian persons and congregations in Jamaica, 1896. [By E. Nuttall, Bishop of Jamaica]. [*Kingston,* 1896]

801—NATION BUILDING : a Paradox [a sermon]. By Rev. H. M. F. MacDermot. Reprinted from the "Jamaica Churchman." [*Kingston.*] 1899

802—CHRIST'S GREAT COMMISSION AND THE WORK IN JAMAICA : A sermon preached at the opening of the Synod of the Presbyterian Church of Jamaica, at Lucea, January 24th, 1899, and printed by order of the Synod. By the Rev. John Robson, M.A., D.D. *Kingston,* 1899

803—WOMAN : Her sphere and opportunities. [a sermon]. By Rev. William Graham, Scotch Kirk, Kingston. *Kingston,* 1899

804—A SERMON preached by the Archbishop of the West Indies [E. Nuttall] at the Parish Church, St. Andrew, Halfway-Tree, on Sunday morning, 31st December, 1899. 1900

805—SERMON (printed by request) preached by Rev. W. Graham at the Scotch Kirk, Sunday evening, June 10th, in connection with the public celebrations on the fall of Pretoria. *Kingston,* [1900]

806—THE RELIEF OF LADYSMITH. A sermon delivered at the Scotch Kirk,

Duke Street, Kingston, on Sunday night, 3rd March, 1900. By the Rev. W. Graham. *Kingston,* 1900

807—SERMON preached at St. Luke's Cross Roads, by the Rev. B. J. Shaul. The Entry into Pretoria. *Kingston,* 1900

808—THE LORD'S DAY. A Sermon preached in substance in St. Mary's Church, Port Maria, by the Rev. John H. H. Graham, Rector. [1901]

809—IN THE BEGINNING; or notes on Genesis. By R. E. Clarke. *Kingston* 1900

81(—OUT OF EGYPT; or Notes on Exodus. By R. E. Clarke. *Kingston,* 1901

811—IN MEMORIAM SERMON [Queen Victoria]. Scotch Church, Duke Street, Kingston, by Rev. W. Graham, on Sunday 27th January, 1901. *Kingston,* [1901]

812—PASTORAL LETTER of the Archbishop and Bishops of the Church of England in the Province of the West Indies, 1901. *Kingston,* 1901

XIII. POETRY AND THE DRAMA.

813—*POEM PANIGYRICAL on His Grace the D. of Albermale, with remarks on his voyage for Jamaica and the late Treasure brought home in the James and Mary. 1686

8 4—*THE POLITICKS AND PATRIOTS OF JAMAICA. A poem. *London,* 1718

815—JAMAICA. A Poem in three parts. Written in that island in the year MDCCLXXVI, to which is annexed a Poetical Epistle from the Author in the island to a friend in England. *London,* 1777

816—*THE ELECTION, a poem. *Kingston,* 1788

817—WRONGS OF ALMOONA, or the African's Revenge. A narrative poem, founded on historical facts. By a Friend to all mankind. *Liverpool,* [1788]

8 3—LAYS OF THE SEA and other poems. By Mrs. Henry Lynch. 2nd ed. *London,* 1850

8 9—THE LAST LAYS OF SHILOAH. By [Rev.] J[ohn] Radcliffe. *London,* 1874

820—THE ISLE OF STREAMS or the Jamaica Hermit and other poems. By William Hosack. *Edinburgh,* 1876

821—MALCOLM AND ALONZO, OR THE SECRET MURDER OF LEONARD: a Tragedy in five acts. By John Duff Spraggs. [*Kingston*] *Jamaica,* 1880

822—DON JUAN IN JAMAICA: in two cantos. By Nemo. *Kingston,* n.d. [after 1881].

823—ROUND THE ISLAND. In three cantos. By Titus A. Brick, *Kingston,* 1882

824—WATCHMEN IN CONFERENCE, an idyll of the Protest. By the Rev. D. R. Morris, formerly Rector of St. James, Jamaica. *Sandow·,* *I. of W.* n. d.

825—JAMAICA, a poem. By T[om] R[edcam] [T. H. MacDermot], a Jamaican. *Kingston,* 1889

826—VIRGINIE: A tale of the Slave-Trade, and other poems. By Alexander MacGregor James. *Kingston,* 1895

827—TO HER MOST GRACIOUS MAJESTY VICTORIA Queen and Empress; who, as the greatest Sovereign of the British Empire and the best of women, will for ever live in the hearts of her loyal and loving subjects throughout the world. These Stanzas as written in commemoration of the sixtieth anniversary of her accession to the Throne are humbly and respectfully inscribed and addressd by Her Majesty's most dutiful subject and servant, E. N. McLaughlin. *Spanish-Town,* [1897]

828—POEMS. By Rose Delisser. Pamphlet dedicated to the Canadian War Fund. *Kingston,* [1900]

XIV.—SOCIOLOGY.

829—*THE GROANS OF JAMAICA, expressed in a letter from a gentleman residing there, to his friend in London, containing a . . . narrative of some of the crying grievances and . . . oppressions which gave , . rise to the present . . discontents . . . among the Inhabitants of that Island, etc. *London,* 1714

830—A LETTER FROM A CITIZEN of Port Royal in Jamaica to a citizen of New York relating to some extraordinary measures lately set on foot in that Island. *Dublin*, printed. *London*, reprinted,   1756

831—*A ROLAND FOR AN OLIVER . . . By Dr. Dancer. *St. Jago de la Vega*,   1809

832—THE PRESENT RUINOUS SITUATION of the West India Islands, submitted to the people of the British Empire ; with a few remarks upon the imposition and oppressions under which the merchants and planters of those Islands have long suffered.. By a Native of Jamaica. *London*,   [1811]

833—*DREAMS OF DULOCRACY, or the puritanical obituary. "An Appeal" not to the romantic sensibility, but to the good sense of the British Public. By the Reverend George Wilson Bridges . . . *Jamaica*, 1824

834—STATE OF LAW AND MANNERS in Jamaica, illustrated, by the accounts given in the Christian Record of that island of the conduct of Councils of Protection and of the Minutes of Evidence in the case of the Rev. Mr. Bridges and his slave Kitty Hylton. n. d.

835—A REPLY to the Speech of Dr. Lushington in the House of Commons on the 12 June, 1827, on the condition of the free-coloured people of Jamaica. *London*,   1828

836—*A LETTER to the proprietors and mortgagees of estates in the island of Jamaica : on promoting immigration into that colony. By A. A. Lindo. *London*,   1836

837—REPORT of Captain J. W. Pringle on Prisons in the West Indies. Part I., Jamaica. Parliamentary Papers. *London*,   1838

838—A REPLY to the Letter of the Marquis of Sligo to the Marquis of Normanby relative to the present state of Jamaica. By William Burge. *London*,   1839

839—RECONCILIATION respectfully recommended to all parties in the Colony of Jamaica in a letter addressed to the Planters by Joseph John Gurney. *Kingston*,   1840

840—*REMARKS on emigration to Jamaica addressed to the Coloured Classes of the United States. *London*,   1840

841—*NOT A LABORER WANTED IN JAMAICA. By T. Clarkson.   1842

842—*A BRIEF ENQUIRY into the condition of Jamaica. By Thomas Jelly. *London*,   1847

843—STATEMENT OF FACTS relative to Jamaica. *London*,   1852

844—SUGGESTIONS relative to the improvement of the British West Indian Colonies by means of instruction by Ministers of Religion and Schools. The Relations of Property and Labour. Agricultural and other Industrial Improvements, &c., &c., with especial reference to the increased cultivation of the Sugar Cane and Cotton in Jamaica and British Guiana. By a resident in the West Indies for thirteen years. With an introduction and concluding remarks by a late Stipendiary Magistrate in Jamaica [Stephen Bourne]. *London*,   1853

845—THE "RUIN" OF JAMAICA. By R. Hildreth. (Anti-Slavery Tracts No. 6). *New York*, n. d. [?1855]

846—FIRST ANNUAL REPORT OF THE ST. GEORGE'S HOME AND REFORMATORY FOR BOYS, established in Kingston. . . 1858. *Kingston*, 1859

847—THE PROBLEM OF JAMAICA. Reprinted from the "Eclectic Review" [By a thirty years' resident]. n. d. [1865]

848—THE EXPOSITION OF ABUSES IN JAMAICA. By Dr. E. B. Underhill. (n. d.)

849—*A LETTER addressed to Right Hon. E. Cardwell. By Dr. Edward Bean Underhill. With illustrative documents on the condition of Jamaica, and an Explanatory Statement. *London*,   1865

850—DR. UNDERHILL'S TESTIMONY ON THE WRONGS OF THE NEGRO IN JAMAICA, EXAMINED ; in a letter to the Editor of the Times. [By Abraham Lindo]. *Falmouth, Ja.*, [1866]

851—ENGLAND AND HER SUBJECT RACES, with special reference to Jamaica. By Charles Savile Roundell, M.A. *London*,   1866

852—*JAMAICA, its state and prospects, with an exposure of the proceedings of the Freedman's Aid Society and the Baptist Missionary Society. ·*London*,   1867

853—*WOMEN'S RIGHTS : a lecture delivered in Kingston by S. Powell Thomson (of British Guiana). 2nd ed. *Kingston*,   1876

854—LABOUR, PAUPERISM, CRIME. A short view of the present state of things in Jamaica. [By William Ewen]. *Kingston*,   1877

855—MANNERS AND CUSTOMS of the Country a generation ago. By Henry G. Murray. From Kittle's Wake, being the second of a series of Readings delivered in Kingston and elsewhere. *Kingston*,   1877

856—REPORT of the Commissioners of Enquiry upon the condition of the Juvenile Population of Jamaica, with the evidence taken and an appendix : presented October, 1879. *Kingston*,   1879

857—REMARKS on the Kingston Benefit Building Society, shewing its past working, present condition and its future prospects, with suggestions for its management as regards bonuses to shares, alms houses, &c. the result of careful calculations and much thought. By Geo. Henderson. *Kingston*.   1881

858—FIRST ANNUAL REPORT of the Kingston and Liguanea Charity Organization Society, 1883. *Kingston*,   1884

859—THE CROWN COLONIES OF GREAT BRITAIN. An enquiry into their social condition and methods of administration. By C. S. Salmon. With a chapter on the " Black and Brown Landholder of Jamaica " By R. G. Haliburton, Q.C. . . . *London and Paris*, n. d. [after 1886]

860—THOUGHTS on the condition of Jamaica. By Nil Desperandum. 1887

861—JAMAICA'S GREATEST NEED. By Rev. R. Dingwall. *Christiana, Jamaica*,   1892

862—THE HISTORY of the Royal Lodge No. 207; Dist. No. 1, Kingston, Jamaica. By Eml. X. Leon. *Kingston*,   1894

863—THE HISTORY of the Friendly Lodge No. 239, District No. 2, Kingston, Jamaica. By Eml. X. Leon. *Kingston*,   1998

864—BLACK JAMAICA. A study in Evolution. By W[illiam] ·P[ringle] Livingstone. *London*,   1899

XV.—FOLK LORE.

865—LECTURES on Negro Proverbs, with a preliminery paper on negro literature. By Rev. J[ohn] Radcliffe. *Kingston*,   1869

866—STORIES ABOUT [Jamaica]. By Lady Barker, with illustrations. New ed. *London*,   1871

867—MAMMA'S Black Nurse Stories : West Indian Folk-Lore. By Mary Pamela Milne-Home [née Ellis]. With illustrations. *Edinburgh & London*,   1890

868—A DAY WITH JOE LENNAN the Rosewell Duppy Doctor and Tommy Silvera or Suck o' Peas Sil. A Lecture delivered by W. C. Murray at the Conversorium in February, 1889. *Kingston*,   1891

869—JAMAICA SUPERSTITIONS : or the Obeah Book. A complete treatise of the absurdities believed in by the people of the island. By R. T. Banbury. *Kingston*,   1895

870—JAMAICA PROVERBS AND JOHN CANOE ALPHABET. Illustrated by Miss [Violet] Heaven. *Kingston*, [1896]

871—THE NEGRO ALPHABET. By V[iolet] Heaven. *Kingston*,   [1897]

872—ANNANCY STORIES. By Pamela Colman Smith. [Illustrated by the authoress]. *New York*,   1899

873—A SELECTION OF ANANCY STORIES. By " Wona " [Una Jeffrey-Smith]. *Kingston*,   1899

874—A WEEK'S RAMBLING WITH " BRA QUAMIN." By W. C. Murray. *Savanna la-Mar*,   1900

XVI.—FICTION.

875—PEREGRINATIONS OF JEREMIAH GRANT, ESQ., the West Indian. *London*,   1763

876—MONTGOMERY ; or the West Indian Adventurer. A Novel in three volumes, by a gentleman resident in the West Indies. 3 vols. *King-ston,* 1812-1813

877—THE KOROMANTYN SLAVES, or West Indian Sketches. By the author of " The Solace of an Invalid." *London,* 1823

878—HAMEL, THE OBEAH MAN [of Jamaica]. 2 vols. *London,* 1827

879—MARLY ; or Life of a Planter in Jamaica : comprehending characteristic sketches of the Present State of Society and Manners in the British West Indies and an impartial review of the leading questions relative to Colonial Policy. 2nd ed. *Glasgow, Liverpool and London,* 1828

880—*TOM CRINGLE'S LOG. [By Michael Scott.] *Philadelphia,* 1833
The same. Edinburgh, 1834
[*Many later editions.*]

881—*THE CRUISE OF THE MIDGE. [By Michael Scott.] *Edinburgh,* 1834
[*Many later editions.*]

882—OLD PORT ROYAL or the Buccaneers' Home : An Historical Novel. By Samuel Gray. 2 vols. [vol. I. only in Library]. *Kingston,* 1841

883—THE COTTON-TREE ; or Emily the little West Indian. A tale for young people. By Mrs. Henry Lynch [née Ellen Foulks]. *London,* 1847

884—THE FAMILY SEPULCHRE : a Tale of Jamaica. Illustrated by A. Cooper, R.A., and A. W. Cooper. By Mrs. Henry Lynch. *London,* [1848]

885—MAUDE EFFINGHAM : a Tale of Jamaica. By Mrs. Henry Lynch. *London,* 1849

886—CHARLES VERNON : a transatlantic tale. By Lieut.-Col. Henry Senior. 2 vols. *London,* 1849

887—THE MOUNTAIN PASTOR. By Mrs. Henry Lynch. *London,* 1852

888—THE WONDERS OF THE WEST INDIES. By Mrs. Henry Lynch. *London,* 1856

889—COUSIN STELLA, OR CONFLICT. By the author of ' Violet Bank and its inmates.' [Mrs. Jenkin née Jackson]. 3 vols. *London,* 1859

890—THE CAPTAIN'S STORY ; or Jamaica sixty years since. By Captain Brooke-Knight. With illustrations by John Gilbert. *London,* n. d. [first published in the " Leisure Hour." 1859-60]

891—*THE MAROON. With illustrations. By Captain Mayne Reid. *London,* 1862
Many later editions.

892—CAPTAIN CLUTTERBUCK'S CHAMPAGNE. A West Indian Reminiscence. Originally published in Blackwood's Magazine. *Edinburgh and London,* 1862

893—VERE OF " OURS,', the Eighth or King's. By James Grant. 3 vols. *London,* 1878

894—POOR LITTLE LIFE : a Family Episode. By George Temple. From " Chambers's Journal," 1883

895—IN ALL SHADES : a Novel. By Grant Allen. 3 vols. *London,* 1886

996—A STUDY IN COLOUR. By " Alice Spinner" [Mrs. Fraser, née Webb]. 2nd ed. *London,* 1894

897—LUCILLA : an Experiment. By " Alice Spinner" [Mrs. Fraser, née Webb]. *London,* 1895

898—A RELUCTANT EVANGELIST AND OTHER STORIES. By " Alice Spinner" [Mrs. Fraser, née Webb]. *London,* 1896

899—THE WOOINGS OF JEZEBEL PETTYFER : being the personal history of Jehu Sennacherib Dyle commonly called Masheen Dyle : together with an account of certain things that chanced in the house of the Sorcerer. By Haldane Macfall. *London,* 1898

900—NEGRO NOBODIES ; being a series of sketches of peasant life in Jamaica. By Noël de Montagnac. (Overseas Library.) *London,* 1899

901—A DAUGHTER OF ENGLAND. By May Crommelin. *London,* 1902

902—THE COURT OF DESTINY. By C. G. Chatterton. *London,* 1902

XVII.—WORKS OF REFERENCE.

903—JAMAICA ALMANAC. 1751-1880. Years missing, 1752-1781, 1786, 1787, 1792, 1810, 1834-37, 1843,

1852-54, 1856, 1858-59, 1863. *Kingston.*   1751-1880
[*In 1881, the Handbook of Jamaica first appeared. See No. 914*].

904—MEMBERS OF THE ASSEMBLY OF JAMAICA, from the institution of that Branch of the Legislature to the present time. Arranged in Parochial Lists. By John Roby. *Montego Bay,*   1831

905—JAMAICA GAZETTE AND SUPPLEMENT, 1845 to 1901. 69 vols. (Incomplete). *Jamaica,*   1845-1901

906—AN ALPHABETICAL CATALOGUE of the Books in the Library of the Honble. House of Assembly of Jamaica. *St. Jago de la Vega,* 1852

907—JAMAICA BLUE BOOKS, 1852 to 1854, 1857, 1862, 1866 to 1900-01. *Jamaica,*   1852-1901

908—CATALOGUE of Books and Rules and Regulations of the Colonial Literary and Reading Society, to the 1st July, 1864. *Kingston,* 1864

909—CATALOGUE of the Library of the Assembly of Jamaica. Published by order of the Library Committee. *Spanish Town,*   1865

910—SUMMARY of Census Returns, 1871

911—RULES of the Jamaica Civil Service Mutual Guarantee Association with reference to Law 45 of 1872, approved by the Governor in Privy Council on the 23rd August, 1872, and 2nd November, 1875. *Kingston.*

912—PUBLIC LIBRARY, Jamaica. Catalogue of Works arranged according to subjects. [With manuscript additions]. *Jamaica,*   [ab. 1878]

913—JAMAICA. The Governor's Report on the Blue Book, and Departmental Reports, 1879-80—1895-96. 16 vols. *Kingston,*   1881-1897

The same [without Governor's Report, for which see No. 925] Departmental Reports, 1896-97—1899-1900. 4 vols. *Kingston.*   1898-1901

914—HANDBOOK OF JAMAICA, comprising Historical, Statistical and General Information concerning the Island. Compiled from Official and other reliable Records. 21 vols.

Vols. for 1881 to 1889-90 compiled by A. C. Sinclair and Laurence R. Fyfe; 1890-91 to 1897 by S. P. Musson and T. Laurence Roxburgh; 1898-1902 by T. L. Roxburgh and J. C. Ford. *Jamaica and London,*   1881-1902

915—CHRONOLOGICAL HISTORY OF JAMAICA. By A. C. Sinclair and Laurence R. Fyfe. Extracted from the Handbook of Jamaica for 1882. *Kingston,*   1882

916—BY-LAWS of the Jamaica Masonic Library. *Kingston,*   [1884]

917—CATALOGUE of General Works in the Library of the Institute of Jamaica. *Kingston,*   1887
The same. CATALOGUE OF WORKS added to the Library of the Institute of Jamaics during the financial year 1887-88. *Kingston,*   1889

918—CHRONOLOGICAL HISTORY OF JAMAICA during the Government of His Excellency Sir Henry Wylie Norman, G.C.B., G.C.M.G., C.I.E. By A[ugustus] C[onstantine] Sinclair and L[aurence] R. Fyfe. *Jamaica,*   1889

919—CATALOGUE of the Books in the Library of the Victoria Institute, Kingston, Jamaica. *Kingston,* 1891

920—CENSUS OF JAMAICA AND ITS DEPENDENCIES, 1891. *Kingston,* 1892

921—GENERAL GUIDE to the Museum of the Institute of Jamaica. By T. D. A. Cockerell, F.Z.S., F.E.S. *Kingston,*   1893

922—BIBLIOTHECA JAMAICENSIS. Some account of the principal works on Jamaica in the Library of the Institute. By Frank Cundall, F.S.A. (Reprinted from "The Handbook of Jamaica for 1895") *Kingston,*   1895

923—CATALOGUE OF BOOKS in the Library of the Institute of Jamaica. Arranged under authors' names and under titles. [Compiled by Frank Cundall]. *Kingston,* 1895

923a—OFFICIAL AND OTHER PERSONAGES OF JAMAICA, from 1655 to 1790; to which is added a chapter on the Peerage, &c. in Jamaica compiled from various sources. By W[alter] A[ugustus] Feurtado. *Kingston,*   1896

924—The Handbook of the Turks and Caicos Islands. Being a compendium of History, Statistics and general information concerning the islands from discovery to the present time. By [Rev.] J. Henry Pusey. *Kingston,* 1897

925—Jamaica. Annual Reports [Governor's] for 1895-96, 1896-97, 1897-98, 1898-99, 1899-1900. Presented to both Houses of Parliament. *London,* 1897-1901

926—The Sub-Officers' Guide Containing Definitions of Crimes. Forms of Informations and Proclamations, and an Index to Criminal Laws, for use by Sub-Officers of Police: approved by Honble. Thomas Bancroft Oughton, Acting Attorney-General. Compiled, with the authority of the Inspector General of Police, by Harry McCrea, Inspector of Police. *Kingston,* 1900

XVIII. Miscellaneous:

(Including works by Jamaica authors on non-Jamaica subjects.)

927—Poems written chiefly in the West Indies. [By Bryan Edwards.] *Kingston,* 1792

928—The History, Civil and Commercial of the British Colonies in the West Indies. By Bryan Edwards. 2 vols. *London,* 1793 [*Later editions.*]

929—*A Treatise on Magnetism, with a description and explanation of a meridional and azimuth compass, for ascertaining the quantity of variation without any calculation whatever, at any time of the day, also improvements upon compasses in general. With tables of variation for all Latitudes and Longitudes. By Ralph Walker, of Jamaica. [in or bef. 1796]

929a—Poems and Songs on different subjects. By Andrew McKenzie [of Dunover]. *Belfast,* 1810

930—*The Isle of Devils, a Historical Tale founded on an anecdote in the annals of Portugal. By M. G. Lewis, M.P. . . *Kingston* 1827

931—Reports on the intended Lighthouse at Morant Point. Submitted to the Honble. the Commission-

ers for erecting the same. By Alexander Gordon. *Jamaica,* 1841

932—Pickwick in Jamaica. By W. G. Freeman. [Manuscript.]

933—Recollections of West-End Life, with Sketches of Society in Paris, India, &c., &c. By Major Chambre, late 17th Lancers. *London,* 1858

934—Solvitur Ambulando. A Lecture delivered on behalf of the Reading Society, Kingston, April 9th 1870. By the Rev. J. Radcliffe. *London,* 1870

935—Synonyms Discriminated; a complete Catalogue of the Synonymous Words in the English language, with descriptions, quotations, &c. By C. J. Smith, Archdeacon of Jamaica, 1871

936—Objects of the Jamaica Institute. By Rev. John Radcliffe. *Kingston,* 1881

937—The Reconstruction of the City [of Kingston]. A paper read at a meeting of the Fire relief Committee. By the Bishop of Jamaica [E. Nuttall]. *Kingston,* 1882

938—Outlines of a Lecture on Vegetable Chemistry. By J. J. Bowrey, F.C.S., *Kingston,* 1884

939—Independent Order of Good Templars. Journals of the Proceeding of the eleventh annual session of the Grand Lodge of Jamaica, 1887. *Kingston.* 1887

940—The Advantages to result from Railway Extension. By Hon. W. B. Espeut. *Kingston,* 1887

941—Chess: its Poetry and its Prose-A Practical and Theoretical Treatise on the arts of composing and solving Chess Problems. By Arthur F. Mackenzie. With numerous illustrative diagrams. . . . With solutions and critical and explanatory notes; also elementary instructions for beginners. *Kingston,* 1887

942—Kingston Streets Reconstuction. Report of Commission [Valentine G. Bell, Chairman]. *Kingston,* 1887

943—A Lecture on the Panama Canal: its past history and future prespects delivered at the National Theatre of Colon, 10th June, 1889, By A. E. Verdereau *Kingston.* 1889

944—The "Hotels Scheme" examined. With remarks and suggestions supplemented by remarks on the Railway, by a Business Man. n.d.

945—Blackheath and the Story of a Sea Ball or Sink Hole. [By W. Duncan Byles]. *Kingston,* 1890

946—Professor Huxley on "Natural Rights and Political Rights" : a criticism by Alex. M. Mould. *Kingston.* 1890

947 —Correspondence relating to the sale of the Jamaica Railway to an American Syndicate. Presented to Parliament. *London,* 1891

948- Julian the Apostate and other poems. By D[avid] M[orrison] P[anton]. *Cambridge and London,* 1891

949—Institute of Jamaica. Lectures I., Elizabethan Literature, by the Rev. Wm. ~imms, M.A., 1891. II., The Physiography of Jamaica, by John Stuart, M.A., 1892. III., Hygiene, by Surgeon-Major Barker, M.B., 1892. [Extracted from "Gleaner" newspaper.] 1891-1892

950—Catalogue of the Competitive and Loan Fine Art Exhibition held at the Institute of Jamaica, March, 1892. *Kingston,* 1892

951—The Jamaica Cookery Book. Three hundred and twelve simple Cookery Receipts and household hints, collected by C[aroline] S[ullivan]. *Kingston,* 1893
   The same. 2nd ed. *Kingston,* 1897

952—Night Fighting. A translation from the Russian. By Major-General H[arcourt] M[ortimer] Bengough. 2nd. ed. *London,* 1893

953—Report on Condition of the Jamaica Railway Extensions. By A. M. Wellington, and Report of Messrs. Elliott and Lazarus. 1893

954—Journal of the Institute of Jamaica (for the encouragement of Literature, Science and Art). Vol. I. (1891-1893). Vol. II. (1894-1899). [Edited by Frank Cundall]. *Kingston,* 1894 & 1899

955—Address delivered by the Bishop of Jamaica, Primate of the Province of the West Indies [E. Nuttall], at a meeting of the Bishops of the Provincial Synod and of the Clergy and Laity, Georgetown, Demerara, on Tuesday, March 5th, 1895, *Kingston,* 1895

956—First Choral Competition in Jamaica, 1895. Prospectus. *Kingston,* 1895

957—Museum Work in Jamaica. By J. E. Duerden. Reprinted from "Natural Science," 1896

958—Thoughts on Modern Tactics. By Major-General H. M. Bengough, C. B. *London,* [1896]

959—Sollas' Theatrical Souvenir. [1897]

960—Report on Street Pavements and Tramway construction in the United States and Trinidad, with recommendations for Street Reconstruction in Kingston, prepared for the Kingston Improvement Commissioners. By Alfred G. Nash, C.E., B.Sc. F.R.S., Edin. *Kingston,* 1897

961—The Jamaica Cricket Annual for 1897. Compiled by F. L. Pearce and T. Laurence Roxburgh. *Kingston,* 1897

962—Report on the construction, equipment and working of the Jamaica Railway. By R. Elliott Cooper, M. Inst. C. E. With appendices, plans and diagrams. *London,* 1899

963—When will the XIXth Century end and the XXth begin. Reprinted from "The Gleaner." By Equilibrium [Rev. Horace Scotland]. *Kingston,* 1899

964—Presentation of a Portrait of the Rev. Dr. Gillies to the Directors of the Mico Training College. *Kingston,* 1901

965—Catalogue of Fine Art Loan Exhibition open December 18th to 28th, 1901. *Kingston,* 1901

966—Thirteen Short Lectures on Modern Battles in connection with Fortifications and Tactics from French and German Military Writers, by Maj.-Genl. H. Jardine Hallowes, Commanding the Troops, Jamaica. *Kingston,* 1899

967—Chants du Sauveteur (Sauver ou périr). (Poésie). Par Dathan de Saint-Cyr [of Jamaica]. *Paris,* 1900

968—Etude sur l'Hygiene Publique . . . Par Dathan de Saint-Cyr [of Jamaica]. *Paris,* 1900

969—L'Humanite (Poëme) par Dathan de Saint-Cyr [of Jamaica]. 3me édition. *Kingston,* [1901]

970—Present Day Pamphlets. (i) Spiritualism : its origin and character. (ii) The Medium and the Witch (an appeal to Spiritualists). (iii) Irvingism and the gifts of the Holy Ghost. (iv) The Advance of Rome. By D[avid] M[orrison] Panton. *London,* 1901

MAGAZINE ARTICLES.

(In Magazines published outside Jamaica.)

999—JAMAICA. By Herbert T. Thomas. In "*Journal of the Society of Arts.*" Feb., 1902.

V. BIOGRAPHY.

1000—A LITTLE-KNOWN JAMAICA NATURALIST, DR. ANTHONY ROBINSON. By T. D. A. Cockerell. In the "*American Naturalist,*" 1894

1001—THE CASE OF GOVERNOR EYRE. By J. B. Atlay. In "*The Cornhill Magazine.* February," 1902

VI. i. ZOOLOGY.

1002—*NOTES FROM THE WEST INDIES. By R. H——l [Hill]. In the "*Field Naturalist.*" 1833

1003—*THE ALLIGATOR OF THE ANTILLES. By R. H——l [Hill]. In the "*Field Naturalist.*" 1833

1004—*ON THE BURROWING OWL. By R. H——l [Hill]. In the "*Field Naturalist.*" 1833

1005—*THE GREEN TODY (*Todus viridus*), with a coloured figure. By R. H—l [Hill], with additions, by the Editor [James Rennie]. In the "*Field Naturalist.*" 1833

1006—*OBSERVATIONS of the Nests of the Birds of Jamaica. By Richard Hill. In "*Proceedings of the Zoological Society.*" 1841

1007—*DONATION of Bird's Skins from Jamaica. By Richard Hill. In the "*Proceedings of the Zoological Society.*" 1844

1008—*ON TROCHILUS MARIA. By Richard Hill. In the "*Annals and Magazine of Natural History.*" 1849

1009—*ON MINIUS ORPHEUS. By Richard Hill. In the "*Proceedings of the Academy of Natural Science, Philadelphia.*" 1863

1010—*NOTE on Geotrygon sylvatica. By Richard Hill. In "*Proceedings of the Academy of Natural Science, Philadelphia,*" 1863

1011—NOTES on the Natural History of the Scorpion. By the Hon. Richard Hill, of Jamaica, W. I. (communicated by T. Bland). In the "*Annals of the Lyceum of Natural History of New York.*" October, 1866

1012—*ADDITIONAL NOTES on the Natural History of the Scorpion. By Richard Hill. In the "*Annals of the Lyceum of Natural History, New York.*" 1867

1013—NOTICE of a small collection of Coleoptera from Jamaica, with descriptions of new species from the West Indies. By Charles O. Waterhouse. In the "*Transactions of the Entomological Society.*" 1878

1014—ON A SMALL COLLECTION of Lepidoptera from Jamaica. By Arthur G. Butler, F.L.S., F.Z.S. In the "*Proceedings of the Zoological Society of London.*" 1878

1015—DESCRIPTION of a new species of the genus *Natalus* (Vespertilionidæ) from Jamaica. By G. E. Dobson, M.A. In the "*Proceedings of the Zoological Society.*" 1880

1016—A CATALOGUE of the Fishes received from the Public Museum of the Institute of Jamaica, with Descriptions of *Pristipoma approximans* and *Tylosurus euryops*, two new species. By Tarleton H. Bean, U. S. National Museum, and H. G. Dresel, U.S.N. In the "*Proceedings of United States National Museum.*" 1884

1017—OBSERVATIONS on the Birds of Jamaica, West Indies. By W. E. D. Scott. In "*The Auk,*" published by the American Ornithologists' Union. 1892

1018—THE SMALL GREY SLUG IN JAMAICA. By T. D. A. Cockerell. In "*The Nautilus.*" 1893

1019—A NEW ATTID SPIDER FROM JAMAICA. By T. D. A. Cockerell. In the "*Canadian Entomologist.*" 1893

1020—SLUGS INJURING COFFEE. By T. D. A. Cockerell. In "*The Nautilus.*" 1893

1021—LIST OF THE DIPTERA OF JAMAICA, with descriptions of new species. By Charles W. Johnson. In "*Natural Science of Philadelphia.*" 1894

1022—A SUPPLEMENTARY NOTE to Mr. Johnson's List of Jamaican Diptera. By T. D. A. Cockerell. In "*Natural Science of Philadelphia.*" 1894

1023—DESCRIPTION OF A NEW GENUS and four new species of Crabs from the West Indies.   By Mary J. Rathbun.   In "*Proceedings of U. S. National Museum.*"   1897

1024—A COLLECTION OF FISHES made by Joseph Seed Roberts in Kingston, Jamaica.   By David Starr Jordan and Cloudsley Rutter. From the "*Proceedings of the Academy of Natural Sciences of Philadelphia.*"   1897

1025—THE MONGOOSE IN JAMAICA.   By C. W. Willis.   In "*Popular Science Monthly.*"   Nov.,   1898

1026—ZOOLOGICAL JAMAICA.   By Hubert Lyman Clark.   In "*Natural Science.*"   18·8

1027—THE JAMAICAN SPECIES OF PERIPATUS.   By M. Grabham & T. D. A. Cockerell.   In "*Nature.*"   1901

1028—NEW JAMAICAN UROCOPTIDÆ. By Henry Vendryes.   In "*The Nautilus.*"   May,   1901

1029—RELATIONSHIPS of the Rugosa (Tetracoralla) to the living Zoantheae.   By J. E. Duerden.   In the "*John Hopkins University Circulars.*"   January,   1902

VI. ii.   BOTANY.

1030—*FLORA JAMAICENSIS.   By Carl. Gustav Sandmark.   In "*Dissertatio Bibl. reg. Ber.*"   Upsaliae,   1759

The same.   2nd ed.   in "*Linn. Amoen. Acad.* V.*"*,   1760

1031—*PLANTARUM JAMAICENSIUM PUGILLUS.   By Gabriel Elmgren.   In "Bibl. reg. Ber."   *Upsaliae,*   1759

The same.   2nd ed. in "*Linn Amoen.   Acad.* V.*"*   1760

1032—*DESCRIPTION AND USE OF THE CABBAGE-BARK TREE of Jamaica. By William Wright.   In the "*Philosophical Transactions of the Royal Society, London.*"   1777

1033—*DESCRIPTION OF THE JESUITS BARK TREE of Jamaica and the Caribees.   By William Wright.   In the "*Philosophical Transactions of the Royal Society, London,*"   1777

1034—*A BOTANICAL AND MEDICAL ACCOUNT of the *Quassia simaruba,* or tree which produces the cortex simaruba.   By William Wright.   In

the "*Transactions of the Royal Society, Edinburgh.*"   *Edinburgh,* 1778

1035—*AN ACCOUNT OF THE MEDICINAL PLANTS growing in Jamaica.   By William Wright.   In the "*London Medical Journal.*"   *London,*   1787

1036—*Beskrifning pâ et nytt Orteslägte ifran West Indien, Kalladt.   *Hisingera.*   By Carl N. Hellenius. In "*Kongl. svenska Vetenskaps Akademien; Handlingar.*"   *Stockholm,*   1792

1037—*SOME OBSERVATIONS on a collection of ferns from the island of Jamaica.   By Robert Howard.   In the "*Magazine of Natural History.*" *London,*   1838

1038—*AN ACCOUNT of the tree which produces the Hog-gum of Jamaica. By Dr. E .N. Bancroft.   In "*The Journal of Botany.*"   *London,* 1842

1039—*ON A NEW GENUS OF FLACOURTIACEAE, recently detected by Mr. Purdie in Jamaica.   By W. J. Hooker   In the "*Journal of Botany.*"   *London,*   1844

1040—*JOURNAL of a Botanical Mission to the West Indies in 1843. By William Purdie.   In the "*Journal of Botany,*" *London,*   1844

1041—*SOME ACCOUNT of *Exothea oblongifolia* of Dr. Macfadyen (*Hypelate oblongifolia,* Hook).   By W. J. Hooker.   In the "*Journal of Botany.*" *London,*   1844

1042—*DESCRIPTION of a new Melastomaceous plant, discovered in Jamaica by Dr. Macfadyen.   By W. J. Hooker.   In the "*Journal of Botany and Kew Miscellany.*"   *London,*   1849

1043—*NOTES ON THE BOTANY OF JAMAICA, written during a tour from Moneague, in that island, on the 6th of May.   By R. C. Alexander. In the "*Journal of Botany and Kew Gardens Miscellany.*"   *London,* 1850

1044—*SKILDRING AF NATURE PAA JAMAICA.   In "*Almenfattelige Naturskildringer.*"   *Copenhagen,*   1863

1045—*SUPPLEMENT TO THE JAMAICA FERNS recorded in Grisebach's Flora of the British West Indies. By G. S. Jenman.   In the "*Journal of Botany.*"   *London,*   1877

1046—*West Indian Fruits. By J. H. Hart. In "*The Gardeners' Chronicle*." *London*, 1880

I047—*Spondias in Jamaica. By J. H. Hart. In "*The Gardeners' Chronicle*." *London*, 1880

1048—*Sabal umbra culifera in Jamaica. By D. Morris. In "*The Gardeners' Chronicle*." *London*, 1882

1049—*Jamaica Ferns. By G. S. Jenman. In the "*Journal of Botany*" *London*, 1882

1050—*The Home of Laelia Monophylla, N.E. Br. By J. H. Hart, In "*The Gardeners' Chronicle*." *London*, 1885

1051—*On the Jamaica Ferns of Sloane's Herbarium. By G. S. Jenman. In "*The Journal of Botany*." *London*, 1886

1052—*Some additional Jamaica Ferns. By G. S. Jenman. In "*The Journal of Botany*." *London*, 1886

1053—*Pontederia azurea. By J. H. Hart. In "*The Gardener's Chronicle*." *London*, 1887

1054—*Ueber enige Algen aus Cuba, Jamaica und Puerto Rico. Von G. Lagerheim. In "*Botaniska Notiser*." *Lund.*, 1887

1055—Disease of Colocasia in Jamaica. By George Massee. In the "*Journal of the Linnean Society*." *London*, 1887

1056—*Jamaica Mosses and Hepaticae. By Henry Boswell. In "*Journal of Botany*." *London*, 1887

1057—*Cayman Islands. By William Fawcett, B.Sc. In the "*Kew Bulletin*." *London*, 1888

1058—*Jamaica India Rubber. In the "*Kew Bulletin*." *London*, 1888

1059—*Cogwood. In the "*Kew Bulletin*." *London*, 1889

1060—*A Jamaica Drift-fruit. By D. Morris. In "*Nature*." *London*, 1889

1061—*Sur un nouveau parasite dangereux de la Vigne, *Uredo Vialae*. Par G. de Lagerheim. In "*Académie royale des Sciences. Comptes rendus*." *Paris*, 1890

1062—*Some Observations on the Bahamas and Jamaica. By J. T. Rothrock. In the "*Proceeding of the American Philosophical Society*." *Philadelphia*, 1891

1063—Synoptical List, with description of the Ferns and Fern-allies of Jamaica. By G. S. Jenman. In the "*Bulletin of the Botanical Department, Jamaica*." *Kingston*, 1890-1898

1064—*A Visit to the West Indies. [Bahamas, Jamaica and Grand Cayman]. Hy A. S. Hitchcock. In the "*Botanical Gazette*." 1891

1065—*List of Plants collected in the Bahamas, Jamaica and Grand Cayman. By Albert T. Hitchcock. In Fourth annual report of the "*Missouri Botanical Garden*." 1893

1066—*Notes on some Fungi collected in Jamaica. By T. D. A. Cockerell. In the "*Bulletin of the Torrey Botanical Club*." *New York*, 1893

1067—Two New Orchids from Jamaica. By William Fawcett. In the "*Journal of Botany*." *London*, 1895

1068—*A Collecting Tour in Jamaica. By William Harris. In "*The Gardeners' Chronicle*." *London*, 1896

1069—Symbolae ad Bryologiam Jamaicensem. By Carl Müller. In "*Bulletin de l'Herbier Boissier*." *Genève*, 1897

1070—*Jamaica, the Fern-lover's Paradise. By B. D. Gilbert. In "*The Fern Bulletin*." *Binghamton, N.Y.* 1897

1071—*Three New Ferns from Jamaica. By B. D Gilbert. In the "*Bulletin of the Torrey Botanical Club*." *New York*, 1897

1072—*The Expedition to Jamaica in the Summer of 1897. By W. K. Brooks. In the "*Johns Hopkins University Circulars*." *Baltimore*, 1897

1073—*List of Cryptogams collected in the Bahamas, Jamaica and Grand Cayman. By Albert S. Hitchcock. In "*The ninth annual report of the Missouri Botanical Garden*." *Missouri*, 1898

1074— *Botanical Aspects of Jamaica. By Douglas Houghton Campbell. In the "*American Naturalist.*" Boston,   1898

1074a—The Algae of Jamaica. By Frank Shipley Collins. In "*Proceedings of the American Academy of Arts and Sciences.*" Nov.   1901

1075—The Botanical Gardens of Jamaica. By John W. Harshberger. In "*The Plant World.*" March,   1902

VI. iii. Geology.

1076—Notice on the Temperature of the Surface Water of the Atlantic observed during a voyage to and from Jamaica. By H. T. de la Beche, F.R.S. In the "*Annals of Philosophy.*"   1825

1077—Notice on the Diluvium of Jamaica. By H. T. de la Beche, F.R.S. In the "*Annals of Philosophy.*"   1825

1078—Remarks on the Geology of Jamaica. By H[enry] T[homas] de la Beche. In the "*Transactions of the Geological Society of London.*" 2nd Series. pt. 2nd. *London*, 1827

1079—On some Cretaceous Rocks in the South-Eastern portion of Jamaica. By Lucas Barrett, F.G.S. In the "*Proceedings of the Geological Society of London.*" 1st Feb.,   1860

1080—On the Association of Granite with the Tertiary Strata near Kingston, Jamaica. By J. G. Sawkins, Esq., F.G.S. In the "*Proceedings of the Geological Collection.*"   1862

1080a—Jamaica, with remarks on some of the other West Indian Islands. (With map). By Alfred G. Nash, B.Sc., F.R.S.E., F.R.G.S., C.E. In "*The Scottish Geographical Magazine.*" Dec.   1899

VI. iv. Climate.

1081—*Rainfall of Jamaica, 1870-76. By Griffith N. Cox. In "*Journal of the Meteorological Society,*" 1878

VIII. Agriculture and Horticulture.

1082—Agricultural Education. By [Rev.] William Simms. In "*West Indian Bulletin : the Journal of the Imperial Agricultural Department for the West Indies.*" Barbados,   1899

1083—Agricultural Instruction in Agricultural Schools in Jamaica. By William Fawcett, B.Sc. In "*West Indian Bulletin.*" Barbados,   1899

1084—Practical Field Instruction in Jamaica. By William Fawcett. In "*West Indian Bulletin.*" Barbados,   1899

1085—The Prevention of the Introduction and Spread of Fungoid and Insect Pests in the West Indies. By William Fawcett. In "*West Indian Bulletin.*" Barbados,   1899

1086—Observations and Experiments to illustrate the principles of Agriculture in Elementary Schools. By William Fawcett. In "*West Indian Bulletin.*" Barbados,   1900

1087—The Proposed Agricultural Department and Agricultural Teaching in Jamaica. By the Rev. Canon Simms, M.A. In "*West Indian Bulletin.*" Barbados,   1900

1088—Distribution of Economic Plants in relation to Agricultural Development. By William Fawcett, B.Sc. In "*West Indian Bulletin.*" Barbados,   1900

1089—Bee-Keeping in Jamaica. By James Doidge. In "*West Indian Bulletin.*" Barbados,   1900

1090—Agricultural Education and its place in General Education. By Rev. Canon Simms. In "*West Indian Bulletin.*" Barbados,   1901

1091—Teaching the Principles of Agriculture in Elementary Schools. By Hon. Thomas Capper, B.A. In "*West Indian Bulletin.*" Barbados,   1901

1092—Jamaica Fruit Trade. Reprinted from "The Times" of August 30, 1901. In "*West Indian Bulletin.*" Barbados,   1902

1093—The Prospects of the Sugar Industry in Jamaica. By Herbert C. Cousins, M.A. In "*West Indian Bulletin.*" Barbados,   1902

1094—The Teaching of Agriculture in the West Indies : Jamaica. By A. B. McFarlane and W. R. Buttenshaw, M.A. In " *West Indian Bulletin.*" *Barbados,* 1902

1095—The Regulation of the Quality of Exported Fruit. By Hon. Sydney Olivier, C.M.G. In " *West Indian Bulletin.*" *Barbados,* 1902

1096—The Banana Industry in Jamaica. By Hon. William Fawcett. In " *West Indian Bulletin.*" *Barbados,* 1902

X. Law and Politics.

1097—Does Jamaica contain a Lesson in Colonial Government ? By Julius Moritzen. In " *The American Monthly Review of Reviews.*" Oct., 1900

1098—The Legislation of Jamaica, 1900. By S. Leslie Thornton. In the " *Journal of the So iety of Comparative Legislation.*" N.S. VIII., 1901

XIV. Sociology.

1099—A Dress Rehearsal of Rebellion, among the Maroons at Annotto Bay, Jamaica. By Phil Robinson. In " *The Contemporary Review.*" Nov., 1898

1100—The Present Condition of Jamaica and Jamaicans. By T. H. MacDermot. In " *The Canadian Magazine.*" Oct., 1899

1101—The Negro as a Factor in the Future of the West Indies. By H. G. DeLisser. In " *The New Century Review.*" Jan., 1900

1102—The White Man in the Tropics. By H. G. DeLisser. In the " *New Century Review.*" Feb., 1900

1103—Has Jamaica Solved the Color Problem ? By Julius Moritzen. In " *Gunton's Magazine.*" Jan., 1901

XVIII. Miscellaneous.

1104—A Day's Sport in Jamaica In " *Baily's Magazine.*" Sep. 1890

1105—Margaret : A sketch in Black and White. By the author of ' A Study in Colour ' [Mrs. Fraser]. In " *The National Review.*" August, 1894

1106—Library Work in Jamaica. By Frank Cundall. In " *Transactions and Proceedings of the Second International Library Conference held in London, July 13-16.*" 1897

1107—A Woman's Hand. By Grant Allen. In " *The Cosmopolitan.*" Dec. 1898

1108—Fighting a Privateer. [By Col. Henry Senior, 1813]. Edited by Mrs. M. C. M. Simpson. In " *Cornhill.*" Oct. 1900

1109—Adventures and Experiences. Unpublished Letters from Jamaica, written in 1813. By Col. Henry Senior. *Excerpted from* " *The Gleaner.*" *Kingston,* 1902

NEWSPAPERS AND PERIODICALS.

A † is placed before those newspapers which are still in course of publication. The titles and dates of the newspapers which are not in the Library of the Institute are marked * : many of these titles are taken from an article by Mr. George F. Judah in "The Jamaica Times" for 21st Jan., 1899.

1—THE ST. JAGO DE LA VEGA GAZETTE, *Spanish Town*. (*Founded* 1756). Weekly. 1791 (vol. XXXVI) to 1832. 23 vols.

2—ROYAL GAZETTE, *Kingston*. (*Founded* 1779). Weekly. 1780 (vol. II) to 1838, and 1842 (incomplete). 50 vols.

3—JAMAICA MERCURY AND KINGSTON WEEKLY ADVERTISER. *Kingston*. (*Founded* 1779). 1779, 1780. 2 vols.

3a—THE CORNWALL CHRONICLE, OR COUNTY GAZETTE. *Montego Bay*. (*Founded?* 1773). Weekly. 1826. (vol. LIV.) 1 vol.

4—THE DIARY AND KINGSTON DAILY ADVERTISER, *Kingston*. (*Founded* 1795). 1796. (No. 330 et seq). 1 vol.

5—THE COLUMBIAN MAGAZINE, *Kingston*. (*Founded* 1796). Monthly. 1796 to 1800. 8 vols.

6—THE NEW JAMAICA MAGAZINE, *Kingston*. (*Founded about* 1798). Monthly. 1798, 1799. 2 vols.

7—THE JAMAICA MAGAZINE, containing original essays, moral, philosophical and literary . . . . *Kingston*. (*Founded* 1812). Monthly. 1812 and 1813. 4 vols.

8—THE KINGSTON CHRONICLE AND CITY ADVERTISER, *Kingston*. (*Founded about* 1805). Daily. 1818 (vol. XIV.) to 1837 (incomplete). 16 vols.

9—JAMAICA COURANT AND PUBLIC ADVERTISER, *Kingston*. (*Founded about* 1805). 1821 (vol. xvii.), and 1823 and 1828. 2 vols.

10—THE TRIFLER, *Kingston*. (*Founded* 1823). 1823. 1 vol.

11—JAMAICA JOURNAL, *Kingston*. Weekly. (*Founded in* 1823). 1824 (vol. ii.). 1 vol.

12—*THE TRIFLER, *Montego Bay*. (*Founded* 1822. *Merged* in 1826 in *The Gossip*).

13—*THE BUCCATORO JOURNAL. (*Founded about* 1828: *merged* 1832 *in the "Iconoclast."*). Weekly.

14—THE WATCHMAN AND JAMAICA FREE PRESS, *Kingston*. (*Founded about* 1830: *ended* 1865). Bi-weekly. 1830 to 1832. 3 vols.

15—*THE CORNWALL ADVERTISER, *Kingston*. (*Founded about* 1831: *ended about* 1834).

16—JAMAICA DESPATCH AND SHANNON'S DAILY MESSENGER. (*Founded* 1832). *Kingston*, 1834 (No. 497 et seq.) and 1835, (incomplete). 1 vol.

16a—*THE COLONIAL REFORMER, *St. Jago de la Vega*. - (*Founded about* 1832: *ended about* 1843). Weekly.

16b—*THE ICONOCLAST. (*Founded* 1832: *ended* 1839).

17—COMMERCIAL ADVERTISER, *Kingston*. (*Founded* 1833). Daily 1834. 1 vol.

18—†THE GLEANER AND DECORDOVA'S ADVERTISING SHEET, *Kingston*. (*Founded* 1833). Daily. 1866 to 1901. 55 vols.

19—JAMAICA HERALD AND COMMERCIAL ADVERTISER, *Kingston*. (*Founded* 1833). 1835 (vol. iii.) Daily. 2 vols.

20—JAMAICA BAPTIST HERALD AND FRIEND OF AFRICA, *Falmouth*. (*Founded about* 1834: *ended about* 1843). 1841–1843 (vol. iv). 3 vols.

21—FALMOUTH POST AND JAMAICA GENERAL ADVERTISER, *Falmouth*, (*Founded* 1835: *ended about* 1874). Weekly. 1835 to 1874. 41 vols.

22—MORNING JOURNAL, *Kingston*. (*Founded* 1838: *ended* about 1875). 1838 to 1875 (incomplete.) 17 vols.

23—*THE CORNWALL COURIER, *Falmouth*. (*Founded about* 1839: *ended about* 1844.)

24—*PAUL PRY, *St. Jago de la Vega*. (*Founded* 1840 : *ended* 1841). Bi-weekly.

25—*THE MIDDLESEX GAZETTE, *St. Jago de la Vega*. (*Founded about* 1841 : *ended about* 1845).

26 *THE POLYPHEME, *Kingston*. (*Founded about* 1841 : *ended about* 1842). Weekly.

26a—*THE SCORPION, *Kingston* (*Founded about* 1842 : *ended* 1848)· Bi-weekly : then weekly.

27—*THE JAMAICA TIMES, *Kingston*. (*Founded about* 1842 : *ended about* 1844). Daily.

28—*THE STANDARD, *Kingston*. (*Founded about* 1842 : *ended about* 1845.) Daily.

29—*THE REPORTER, *Kingston*. (*Founded and ended* 1843). Daily.

30—*THE OLD HARBOUR MIRROR, *Old Harbour*. (*Founded and ended* 1843). Weekly.

31—JAMAICA MONTHLY MAGAZINE, *Kingston*. (*Founded* 1844). 1844 and 1846 to 1848. 3 vols.

32——*THE ADVERTISING SHEET, *Kingston*. (*Founded about* 1844 : *ended about* 1846). Daily.

33—*THE JAMAICA GUARDIAN AND PATRIOT, *Kingston*. (*Founded about* 1845 : *ended about* 1847). Weekly.

34—COLONIAL STANDARD AND JAMAICA DESPATCH, *Kingston*. (*Founded* 1849 : *ended* 1895). Daily. 1850 to 1895. 57 vols.

35—*THE CHRISTIAN TIMES. (*Founded about* 1849).

36—*THE POLITICAL SATIRIST, *Kingston*. (*Founded* 1849 : *ended* 1851). Weekly.

37—THE DAILY ADVERTISER, *Kingston*. (*Founded* 1850 : *merged in* 1859 *in the* "*Jamaica Tribune*"). 1851 to 1858. (incomplete.) 7 vols.

38—*THE TRELAWNY, *Falmouth*. (*Founded about* 1852).

39—*THE BANNER OF THE PEOPLE, *Kingston*. (*Founded* 1852).

40—*THE CREOLE MISCELLANY. (*Founded about* 1852 : *ended about* 1855).

41—*NUNES'S ADVERTISING SHEET, *Montego Bay*. (*Founded about* 1854 : *ended about* 1874).

42—*GALL'S FAMILY NEWSPAPER, *Kingston*. (*Founded* 1855 : *merged in Galls News Letter*, 1857).

43— GALL'S NEWS LETTER, *Kingston*. Daily. (*Founded* 1857 : *ended* 1899.) 1879 (vol. xxii) to 1899. 38 vols.

44 THE JAMAICA TRIBUNE AND DAILY ADVERTISER, *Kingston*. (*Founded* 1859 : *ended* 1866.) 1859 to 1864 (incomplete.) 7 vols.

45—*HENDERSON'S DAILY ADVERTISER, *Kingston*. (*Founded* 1859 : *became Daily Record* 1860 : *merged in Jamaica Guardian* 1860.)

46—THE JAMAICA DAILY GUARDIAN, *Kingston*. (*Founded* 1860.) 1861 (No. 254 et seq.) to 1871. 11 vols.

47—*THE JAMAICAN, *St. Ann's Bay and Port Maria*. (*Founded about* 1862 : *ended about* 1865). Weekly.

48—THE SENTINEL, *Kingston*. Bi-weekly. (*Founded* 1864 : *ended* 1865). 1864-65. 2 vols.

49—* †THE JAMAICA CHURCHMAN : a monthly journal and review. *Kingston*. (*Founded* 1872 *as the Jamaica Church Chronicle : became Jamaica Churchman in* 1880).

50—†THE BUDGET, *Kingston*. (*Founded* 1874). Tri-weekly. 1874 and 1881-1892. 17 vols.

51—*‡THE NEW CENTURY, *Montego Bay*. (*Founded* 1882 *as* "*The 19th Century and St. James Chronicle*"). Weekly.

52—*THE CREOLE. (*Founded* 1882).

53—EVENING EXPRESS, *Kingston*ʼ (*Founded* 1884 : *ended* 1887). Daily 1885 to 1887. 6 vols.

54—JAMAICA POST AND WEST INDIAN ADVERTISER, *Kingston*. (*Founded* 1887 : *merged in the* "*Jamaica Daily Telegraph*" *in* 1898). Daily. 1887 to 1899. 22 vols.

55—THE WEST INDIAN FIELD : a Weekly Newspaper of Agriculture, Education, Pastime and Sport, *Kingston*. (*Founded* 1885 : *ended* 1886). 1885 and 1886. 2 vols.

56—VICTORIA QUARTERLY, *Kingston.* (*Founded* 1889 : *ended* 1892). Monthly. 1889 to 1892. 5 vols.

57.—*†THE BAPTIST REPORTER, *Kingston.* Monthly.

58—* †THE CORNWALL HERALD. *Montego Bay.* (*Founded* 1895 *at Savanna-la-Mar : removed to Montego Bay* 1900). Weekly.

59—THE JAMAICA CREOLE AND DAILY RECORD, *Kingston.* 1883 (vol. iv). 1 vol.

60*—THE CHRISTIAN HELPER, *Brown's Town.* (*Founded* 1890).

61—THE JAMAICAN, *Kingston.* (*Founded* 1893 : *ended* 1894). Weekly. 1893-94. 1 vol.

62—†WINKLER'S MUSICAL MONTHLY, *Kingston.* (*Founded* 1894 : *ended* 1897 : *revived* 1902). 1894 to 1897. 3 vols.

63—THE EVENING NEWS, *Kingston.* (*Founded and ended,* 1894). Daily. 1 vol. 1894.

64—†JAMAICA ADVOCATE, *Kingston,* (*Founded* 1894). Weekly. 1894 to 1898. 1 vol.

65—*†JAMAICA, *London,* (*Founded* 1894). Issued privately twice a year by the Jamaica Church Association in England.

66—*†CATHOLIC OPINION. *Kingston*' (*Founded* 1895). Monthly.

67—*†THE CATHOLIC MAGAZINE, *Kingston.* (*Founded* 1896). Monthly.

68—†JAMAICA DAILY TELEGRAPH AND ANGLO-AMERICAN HERALD, *Kingston.* (*Founded* 1898 *as successor to* "*Jamaica Post*"). 1898 to 1901. 7 vols.

69 – WINKLER'S CHOIR LEADER, *Kingston.* (*Founded* 1897 : *ended* 1900). Monthly. 1897-1900. 3 vols.

70—†JAMAICA TIMES *Kingston.* (*Founded* 1898). Weekly. 1898 to 1900. 2 vols.

71—*†THE PRESBYTERIAN, *Kingston,* (*Founded* 1900). Monthly.

72—*†JAMAICA UNITED METHODIST MESSENGER, *Kingston.* (*Founded* 1900). Quarterly.

73—†THE JAMAICA JOURNAL OF EDUCATION. (*Founded* 1901). Monthly.

74—†THE TEACHER : a Journal of Education, *Kingston.* (*Founded* 1901). Monthly.

75—*†THE WESLEYAN METHODIST. *Kingston.* (*Founded* 1901). Monthly.

MAPS.

Notes in *italics* have been inserted of events in Jamaica History which have had an effect on its cartography.   The notes between square brackets are not on the maps themselves.

1494. *Jamaica discovered by Columbus.*
1587.　 1. Cuba Insula et Iamaica.   [n.d. ? 1587.   No scale : island 2½ in. long.]
1630.　 2. Insula Iamaica   Scale 1⅜in. =15 miliaria germanica.   [*On same sheet with* Cuba insula, Hispaniola insula, &c. *From "Gerardi Mercatoris Atlas sive Cosmographica Meditationes de Fabrica Mundi et Fabricati Figura, primum à Gerardo Mercatore in choatœ, dinde à Judoco Hondio piae memoriae ad finem perductœ jam vero multis in locis emendatae et de novo in lucem editae.   Ed. decima. Henricus Hondius."   Amsterdami, 1630.*]
　　 3. Cuba Insula et Jamaica.   [n. d.   French edition of No. 2.]
1655. *British Occupation of Jamaica.*
1661.　 4. Map of Jamaica.   Scale 7in.=12 Leagues.   [*In Hickeringill's "Jamaica view'd with all the Ports, Harbours, etc.," 1661.*]
1664 *Modyford's "View of Jamaica" sent to England.*
1671. *Survey made by order of Modyford.*
　"　 4a. Novissima Accuratissima Jamaicæ Descriptio per Johannem Ogiliuum Cosmographum Regium—1671.   F. Lamb. sculp. Scale 1in. = 8 miles.
　"　 5. A New and Exact Mapp of ye Isle of Jamaica as it was lately surveyed by order of Sr. ThomasMediford. Bart. : late Gover. : divided into Precincts, or Parishes, with its Ports, Bayes, etc. Printed for Richard Blome, London, 1671.   Scale 1½ in.=20 miles. [*In " A Description of the Island of Jamaica, &c."   By R. Blome 1672.*]
1671–73.　 6. Isle de la Jamaique diuisée par Paroises ou sont exactement remarques les Ports et les Bayes. Par le Sieur Modiford.   R. Michault scrip.   Scale 1½ in. = 20 miles.   [n. d.   *Copied from Blome's map*].
　"　 7. Nova Designatio Insulæ Jamaicæ ex Antillanis Americæ Septentrion. non postremæ secundum Gubernationes suas accuratas æri incisa et publici juris facta à Matthæo Seuttero, Sac. Cæs. et Reg. Cathol. Maj. Geogr. Augustæ Vindel.   Scale 3⅞ in.= 10 miles.   [n. d.   *Copied from Blome's Map.*]
　　 8. A Map of Jamaica.   Sold by Thomas Bassett in Fleet Street, and Richard Chiswell in St. Paul's Churchyard.   Scale 2½ in. = 30 miles.   [*On one sheet with Barbados.   Description on back.   n. d. Copied from Blome.*]
1673 *Parish of Vere formed.*
1675 *Parishes of St. Thomas-in-the Vale and St. Dorothy formed.*
1677 *Act passed naming the fifteen parishes.*
[? 1680]　 9. Jamaica, Americæ Septentrionalis ampla insula, a Christophoro Columbo detecta, in suas Gubernationes peraccuratè Distincta. Per Nicolaum Visser, Amst : Bat : cum Privilo, ordinm. Generalm. Belgii Fæderati. L. v. Anse schulp. Scale 2 in = 5 miles. [Dutch. n. d.   *Copied from Blome.*]
　　 10. L'Isle de la Jamaique, devisée par Paroisses.   Dressée sur des Memoires Anglois par le Sr de Fer Geographe de sa Mté. Catolie. à Paris.   Scale 3½ in. = 50 miles.   [n. d.   *Copied from Blome.*]
1681 *Act passed confirming the names of the fifteen parishes.*
1675–1693.　 11. A new Map of the Island of Jamaica.   Most humbly inscribed to the Right Honble. Thomas Earl of Stamford, &c.   With inset

map of the harbour of Port Royal. *Part of* **A new map of the English Empire** in the ocean of America or West Indies. Revis'd by I Senex. I Harris Sculp. Scale 3in.= 20 miles. [n. d. : bet. 1675 and 1693.]

11a. A new Mapp of the Island of Jamaica, wherein every Towne, Church, Sugar Worke, Indico Worke, Cotton Workes, Cacao Walke, Craules and Pens for Hoggs and Cattel is described, with the names of the present Proprietors. According to a late Survey thear of P. Lea. With inset maps : I. A new Draught of Port Royal by Anthony Williams. II. A generall Mapp of the Continent and the Islands which bee adjacent to Jamaica. III. The English Empire.

1684. 12. A new and exact Mapp of the Island of Jamaica with ye true and just Scituation of ye severall Townes and Churches and alsoe the Plantations with their names and ye names of ye Proprietors, with amendments of great part of ye sea coast, but more especially ye Harbour of Port Royall, by actuall survey to satisfy such as desire to know ye true Longitude and Latitude of any places mentioned in this map, the latitude of Port Royall was accurately taken by a gnoman of more than 23 foot high and found to bee 17° 32' and its Longitude from London 76° westward or 5 hours and 4 minutes. The characters exprest in ye mapp are for Townes, Churches, Sugar Workes, Indico Workes, Cotton Workes and Provision Plantations, Cacao Walkes, and Craules for Hoggs and Pens for Cattel. Dedicated to Sir Thomas Lynch, Governor, by Charles Bochart and Humphrey Knollis. London. n. d. Scale 5½ in. = 15 miles. [*In " The Laws of Jamcica * * * to which is added The state of Jamaica, as it is now under the Government of Sir Thomas Lynch," London 1684*]

12a Isola de Iames ò Giamaica, possedutta dal Ré Britannico Diuisa in Parrocchie. [n. d. bef. 1693]

1693. *Parish of Kingston formed.*

1693–1703 13. The Island of Jamaica divided into its principal parishes with the roads, &c. By H. Moll, Geographer. Scale 3½ in.= 60 miles. [n. d.]

.‹ 14. Insula Jamaica in suas Parochias divisa, et secundum Exemplar primitivum Londinense excusa. Scale 3⅜ in. = 70 miles. [*Part of* Die Englische Colonie-Laender auf den Insuln von America, und zwar die Insuln S. Christophori, Antego, Jamaica, Barbados. n. d. *Copied from Moll.*]

" 15. A new and accurate map of the island of Jamaica. Divided into its principal parishes. Drawn from surveys and regulated by astronl. observatns. By Eman. Bowen. With inset maps of Harbours of Port Antonio and Kingston. Scale 2¾in. = 30 miles. [n. d.]

1703. *Parish of Westmoreland formed.*

15a. The Island of Jamaica. [*In Hickeringill's " Jamaica Viewed"* 3rd ed., 1705].

15b. L'Isle de la Jamaique divisée par Paroisses. [n. d.]

1723. *Parishes of Portland and Hanover formed.*

1725. 16. A New Map of the Island of Jamaica. With Characters exprest for towns, churches, sugar-works, indico works, cotton and provisions, cacao walks, crawles for hoggs and pens for cattle. *With* the Harbour of Port Royall. Scale 3in.=25 miles. [*In Sloane's "Voyaye to the Islands Madera, Barbados, Nevis, St. Christopher's and Jamaica."* 1725.]

1740. 17. A New Map of the Island of Jamaica. [With Characters expressed in the Map for Towns, Churches, Sugar Works, Indico Works, Cotton, Provision and Cacao Walks, Crawles for Hogs and Pens for Cattle]. With the Harbour of Port Royal. 1740. Scale 3 in. = 25 miles. [*In Leslie's "A New History of Jamaica," 2nd ed. 1740. Copied from Sloane's map.*]

1746. 18. La Jamaïque aux Anglois dans le golfe du Mexique. [and] Bermude. à Paris chez le Sr Le Rouge, 1746. Scale 1in.=20 miles.

1750. 18a. Isle de la Jamaïque. [1750].

1753. 19. A map of the island of Jamaica with exact plans of the Towns of Port Royal and Kingston. By Archibald Bontein, His Majesty's chief Engineer in ye said Island during the late war. Dedicated to H. R. H. William, Duke of Cumberland. Published 1st March, 1753. No scale.

20. Carte reduite de l'isle de la Jamaique pour servir aux vaisseaux du Roy, dressé au Dépost des Cartes et Plans de la Marine en 1753. Par ordre de M. Rouillé, Chr. Comte de Jouy &ca Ministre et Secretaire d'Etat ayant le Departemt. de la Marine. Par le Sr. Bellin, Ingenieur de la Marine et du Depost des Plans, Censeur Royal, de l'Academie de Marine et de la Societé Royale de Londres. J'ay fait une Carte particulière de la Jamaique en plus grand Point et plus detaillée que celle cy. Scale 4in.=11 nautical miles.

1758. 20a. Carte particulière de la Jamaïque dressée au Dépost des Cartes, Plans et Journaux de la Marine pour la Service des Vaisseaux du Roy par ordre de M. le Marquis de Massiac, Lieutenant-General des Armées Navales et Secretaire d'Etat de la Marine. Par le Sr. Bellin . . . 1758. Scale 3 in.=4 nautical miles.

Counties formed.

1759. 21. Carte de l'Isle de la Jamaique. Par le Sr. Bellin, Ingr. de la Marine. 1759. Scale 2 in.=8 French marine Lieues. [*In "Déscription Géographique des Isles Antilles possedées par les Anglois." By Bellin. 1758*].

1762. 21a. Carte de l'isle de la Jamaique. [Par le Sr. Bellin, Paris. 1762]

" 21b. A map of the Island of Jamaica. J. Gibson sculpt. Gent Mag. April 1762. Scale ¾in.=5 leagues.

1763. 21c. *To the Right Honorable George, Earl of Hallifax, one of His Majesty's Principal Secretary's of State, &c., &c. This Map of the Island of Jamaica (laid down from the papers and under the direction of Henry Moore, Esq., His Majesty's Lieutenant-Governor and Commander in Chief of that Island, in the years 1756, 57, 58, 59, 60 and 61, and from a great number of actual Surveys performed by the publishers) is humbly inscribed by His Lordship's most obedient and most humble Servants, Thos. Craskell, Engineer, and Jas. Simpson, Surveyor. D. Fournier direxit, Londini, 1763. Scale, 8 inches = 25 miles.

21d. *To the Right Honorable Wills, Earl of Hillsborough, First Lord Commissioner of Trade and Plantations, this Map of the County of Middlesex in the island of Jamaica . . (as in No. 21c) . . Thos. Craskell, Engineer, and Jas. Simpson, Surveyor. D. Fournier direxit, Londini, 1763. Scale, 2 inches = 3 miles.

21e. *To the Right Honorable Robert, Earl of Holdernesse, This Map of the County of Cornwall in the island of Jamaica . . (as in No. 21c) . . Thomas Craskell, Engineer, and Jas. Simpson, Surveyor. D. Fournier direxit, Londini, 1763. Scale, 2 inches = 3 miles.

21f. *To the Right Honorable George Grenville, Esq., first Lord Commissioner of the Treasury, Chancellor and Under Treasurer of the Exchequer, this Map of the County of Surry in the island of Jamaica . . (as in No. 21c) . . Thomas Craskell, Engineer, and Jas. Simpson, Surveyor. D. Fournier direxit, Londini, 1763. Scale, 2 inches = 3 miles.

1763-1770.   22. Carta rappresentante l'Isola della Giammaica.   D. Ver Rossi
                   M. V. sc. n. d.   Scale 1⅞ in.=8 French marine leagues.
1758-1770.   23. A Chart of the Island of Jamaica with its Bays, Harbours, Rocks,
                   Sounding, &c.   n. d.   Scale 2¼ in.=20 miles.
      "   24. Carte de l'Isle de la Jamaïque.   Par. M. Bonne, Ingénieur-Hy-
                   drographe de la Marine.   n. d.   [1762?] Scale 2¼ in.=32 miles.
      "   25. Carte des Isles de la Jamaïque et de St. Domingue.   n. d.
                   Scale 3½in.=139 statute miles.
      "   25a. La Giammaica.
   1763?   25b. A new map of the Island of Jamaica.   Divided into its Parishes
                   including the South End of Cuba and the West End of His-
                   paniola, with the Trade Winds, &c.   Drawn from the best sur-
                   veys.   By Thos. Kitchin, Geogr.   For the London Magazine.
             25c. A correct map of Jamaica.   B. Cole sculp.   Scale 1 in.=25 miles.
   1767.   26. La Jamaique aux Anglois dans le Golfe du Mexique. à Paris chez
                   Crepy, 1767.   [On same sheet with "La Bermude"].   Scale
                   1¼in.=40 miles.

   1770.   *Parish of Trelawny formed.*

      "   26a. *Carta representante l'isola della Giammaica, 1770.*

1770-1814.   27. A New Map of Jamaica exhibiting the boundaries of each parish
                   and the different Post Roads throughout the island, laid down
                   from the latest surveys.   Scale 2⅓in. = 30 miles.   [With inset
                   map of "A general plan of Port Royal in which the different
                   states of the town are accurately laid down."   n. d.   Scale 1 in.
                   =800 feet.]
   1771.   28. A new Map of Jamaica, in which the several Towns, Forts and
                   Settlements are accurately laid down, as well as the situations
                   and depths of the most noted Harbours and anchoring places,
                   with the limits and boundarys of the different Parishes, as they
                   have been regulated by law or settled by Custom, the greater
                   part drawn or corrected from actual surveys made by Mr. Shef-
                   field and others.   London, 1st Jan., 1771.   Scale 3½ in.=30
                   miles.   [With inset map of " A general plan of Port Royal, in
                   which the different states of the Town [before and after the
                   earthquake] are accurately laid down."]
   1774.   28a. Map of Jamaica, according to a survey made in the year MDCLXX.
                   No scale.   T. Kitchin, sculp.   [*In Long's " History of Jamaica,"*
                   1774.   *Copied from Blome.*]
             28b. Bowles's New one-sheet Map of Jamaica, divided into its Pa-
                   rishes, &c., from the Actual Surveys of Sheffield and others.
                   Printed for the Proprietors Bowles and Carver,   .   .   London.
                   Scale 3in. = 25 miles.   With an inset General Plan of Port
                   Royal in which the different States of the Town are accurately
                   laid down.
   1774.   29. Island of Jamaica.   Divided into Counties and Parishes, accord-
                   ing to the best Authorities.   By Thos. Kitchin, Geogr. Hydro-
                   grapher to His Majesty.   1774.   Scale 4in. = 25 miles.   [*In
                   Long's " History of Jamaica," 1774, and in Browne's " Civil and
                   Natural History of Jamaica," 1789*].

      "   29a. Kaart van het eiland Jamaika.   [Bachiene, 1774.]

   1775.   30. Jamaica, from the latest surveys; improved and enlarged by
                   Thomas Jefferys, Geographer to the King.   London, 20th Feb.,
                   1775.   Scale 3 in. = 25 miles.   With inset Maps of the Har-
                   bours of (i) Kingston and Port Royal, and (ii) Bluefields.   [*In
                   Jeffery's " West Indian Atlas," 1775.*]
   1778.   31. A new and correct Chart of the Island of Jamaica.   With its
                   Bays, Harbours, Rocks, Soundings, &c., 1778.   Scale 3in. = 16
                   miles.   [*In " The English Pilot," 1778.*]

1778. 32. La Jamaique. Dressée sur les derniers Plans. Par Jefferys, traduite de l'Anglais à Paris. With inset Maps of the harbours
of Bluefields, and Kingston and Port Royal.] 1778. Scale
1¼in. = 10 miles.

1779. 33. L'isle de la Jamaique. par M. T. J. [?Monsieur Thomas Jefferys],
Ingénieur Anglois. à Paris, 1779. C. P. R. [With inset Maps
of the Harbours of Bluefields, and Kingston and Port Royal]

" 33a. The Island of Jamaica and Cape Gracias à Dios, with the
Banks. By Thos. Jefferys, Geographer to His Majesty. London, 10th Feb., 1779.

1780. 34. A Chart of the Island of Jamaica with the Bays, Harbours,
Rocks, Soundings, &c. London 31st Aug., 1780, Jno. Lodge,
sculp.

1785. 34a. La Giammaica. [Venice, 1785.]

34b. Carte de l'Isle de la Jamaique. n.d.

1794. 35. A map of the Island of Jamaica, divided into Counties and Par-
ishes for the History of the British West Indies by Bryan
Edwards, Esq., 1794. With explanations of Plantations and
Settlements, Churches and Chapels, Forts and Barracks, Rivers,
Roads, Anchorage for Large and Small Vessels, Parish Boun-
daries, Centre of the Island, and Bryan Castle. 1794. Scale
4in. = 25 miles. [*In Bryan Edwards's " History of the West
Indies," 2nd ed.* 1794.]

" 36. Jamaica from the latest surveys, improved and engraved by
Thomas Jefferys, Geographer to the King. Published 12th
May, 1794. Scale 3¾in. = 30 miles. [With two inset maps :
(1) The harbours of Kingston and Port Royal and (ii) The harbour of Bluefields.]

1799. 36a. Carte de l'Ile de la Jamaïque, extraite des cartes topographiques
angloises de Thos. Craskell, Ingenieur, et de Jas. Simpson, Ar-
penteur, assujetie aux Observations Astronomiques, et rédi-
gée au Dépôt général des Cartes, Plans et Journaux de la Marine et des Colonies en 1786. Corrigée et augmentée en 1799 et
publié par ordre du Ministre de la Marine. [with] Ports de Kingston et de Port Royal. [*Copied from 21c.*]

1803. 37. Jamaica. Exhibiting the Boundaries of each Parish and the
different Post Roads throughout the Island, laid down from the
latest surveys with the Maroon Towns, and seat of the Maroon
War. 1803. Scale 1½in. = 20 miles. [*In Dallas's " History of
the Maroon War," 1803.*]

1804. 38. To His Royal Highness the Duke of York, this Map of the
County of Middlesex in the Island of Jamaica, constructed
from actual surveys under the authority of the Hon. House of
Assembly, by whom it hath been examined and unanimously
approved, is, with permission, most humbly inscribed by His
Royal Highness's faithful and most devoted servant, James
Robertson, A.M. 1804. London, published November 1st, 1804
by James Robertson, A.M., late of Jamaica. Scale 1 in. =1 mile.

" 39. To His Royal Highness, the Duke of Clarence, this Map of the
County of Surrey, in the Island of Jamaica, constructed from
actual surveys, under the authority of the Hon. House of Assembly, by whom it has been examined and unanimously approved, is, with permission, most humbly inscribed by His
Royal Highness's faithful and most devoted servant, James
Robertson, A.M., 1804. London, published November 1st, 1804
by James Robertson, A.M., late of Jamaica. Scale 1 in. = 1
mile.

" 40. To His Royal Highness the Prince of Wales, this Map of the
County of Cornwall in the Island of Jamaica, constructed from

actual surveys, under the authority of the Hon. House of Assembly, by whom it hath been examined and unanimously approved, is, with permission, most humbly inscribed by His
Royal Highness's faithful and most devoted servant, James Robertson, A.M., London, published November 1st, 1804, by James
Robertson, A.M., late of Jamaica. Scale 1 in.= 1 mile.

1804. 41. To the King's Most Excellent Majesty, this Map of the Island
of Jamaica, constructed from actual survey under the authority
of the Hon. House of Assembly, by whom it hath been examined and unanimously approved, is, with His Gracious Permission, most humbly inscribed by His Majesty's most dutiful,
and loyal subject and servant, James Robertson, A.M.. London.
Published Nov. 1st, 1804 by James Robertson, A.M., late of
Jamaica. Scale ½in. = 1 mile.

   [*For these four maps (38-41) a sum of £7,500 was voted to Robertson by the House of Assembly. (Votes 1799-1800, p. 288.)*]

1806. 41a. A new Map of Jamaica exhibiting the boundaries of each Parish
and the different post roads throughout the island, laid down
from the latest surveys. Engraved for Stevenson and Smith's
"New Jamaica Almanac, 1806." [*In the " New Jamaica Almanac, 1806."*]

1807. 42. Jamaica, with Plan of the Town of Kingston. 1807. Scale 2in.
= 25 miles. [*In Renny's " History of Jamaica."*]

1808. 42b. The Island of Jamaica. By W. Heather. 1808. [with inset maps
of the harbours of Savanna-la-Mar, Portland Point, Kingston
and Morant Bay].

1810. 42a. *Jamaica from the latest surveys improved and engraved by Th.
Jeffery. London, 1810.

1814. *Parish of Manchester formed.*

"   43. Jamaica [With inset Maps of the Harbours of Bluefields, and
Kingston and Port Royal]. 1814. Drawn and engraved for
John Thomson & Co's. New General Atlas, 12 August 1814.
Scale 3⅝in. = 30 miles.

1822. 43a. Geographical, statistical and historical Map of Jamaica. Drawn
by J. Finlayson. [Cary and Lea. Philadelphia. 1822.]

1823. 44. Geological Map of Eastern half of Jamaica. By Sir Henry
Thomas de la Beche. 1823. [*In " Remarks on the Geology of
Jamaica, Read before the Royal Geological Society 1825 and 1826."
London, 1827.*]

1825. 44a. Carte géographique, statistique et historique de la Jamaïque.
[Par Buchon, 1825 *Translation of No. 43a.*].

"   44b. Geographisch statistische und historische Charte von Jamaika.
Weimar, 1825. [*Translation of No. 43a.*]

1836. 45. Jamaica with illustrations. The Map drawn and engraved by
J. Rapkin. [n.d.] Scale 2in. = 25 miles. [*In Martin's " British Possessions in the West Indies."*]

1839. 45a. Map of Jamaica compiled chiefly from manuscipts in the Colonial Office and Admiralty, by John Arrowsmith, 1839. [*In "Papers relating to the Labouring Population of the West Indies,"*
1839]. Scale ¾ in. = 5 miles.

1841. *Parish of Metcalfe formed.*

1847. 45b. Map of the Province of Surrey in the Island of Jamaica, constructed from the Maps of the Counties as subdivided into Parishes under Mr. Barclay's Act for the subdivision of the Parishes of the Island, 1st Vic. cap. 34 and 9 Vic. cap. 44, with
numerous additions of Roads, Rivers, Settlements, Mountains,
&c., &c., carefully collected from the large surveys, and this Map
drawn by the orders and under the inspection of the Honourable
House of Assembly in 1846 and 1847, by Edward McGeachy,

Crown Surveyor for the Province of Surrey. M.S. Scale 1 mile = 1 inch.

1847. 45c. Map of the Province of Middlesex in the Island of Jamaica. Is compiled according to the Acts of the Legislature for the subdivision of the Parishes; Passed the 1 and 9 Vic. caps. 34 and 44, and entitled An Act to appoint Commissioners to make a new arrangement of Parishes for their better Civil and Ecclesiastical Government. Drawn by the order of the Honourable House of Assembly in the years, 1846-47 and 48, by John M. Smith, Crown Surveyor, Middlesex. M.S. Scale 1 mile = 1 inch.

[*The set was completed by a third map, of the Province of Cornwall, prepared by John M. Smith in 1846-48; but this has been unfortunately destroyed.*]

1848. 46. Island of Jamaica. Lithographed and printed by W. J. Kidd for P. C. Labatt's " Catechism of the History of Jamaica," 1848, [No Scale. Island 8½ in. long.]

1851. 47. Jamaica. 1851. Scale 1¼ in. = 40 miles. [*In Anderson's "Description and History of the island of Jamaica," 1851.*]

1854. 48. Jamaica [with Moravian Church-stations, with the year of their foundation.] Scale 1⅛ in. = 20 miles. [*In Buchner's " History of the Mission of the United Brethren's Church to the negroes in the island of Jamaica." 1854.*]

1858. 49. Ford and Gall's New Map of Jamaica, showing the Roads, Post Offices, and Shipping Ports, &c. 1858. Scale 4in. = 50 miles. [*In Hill's "Lights and Shadows of Jamaica History," 1859.*]

1860-67. 50. Geological Maps of the Parishes of Jamaica, made in 186'- 1866, by the officers of the Geological Survey of the Island. [*Scale of all ; 1 in. = 1 mile.*]

(a.) Parish of Portland. 1860. W. Metcalfe, litho. Cambridge.

(b.) Parish of Portland. [*Duplicate of (a)*]

(c.) Sections of the Parish of Portland. M S. n.d.

(d.) Parish of St. Thomas-in-the-East, 1861, lith.

(e.) Parish of St. David and part of St. Thomas-in-the-East. By J. G. Sawkins, F.G.S., W.I. Geological Survey, 1861. M.S.

(f.) Parish of St. David. 1861. lith.

(g.) Sections of St. David and western part of St. Thomas-in-the-East. West India Geological Survey, 1861. M.S.

(h.) Parish of Port Royal [*With vertical sections*]. By J. G. Sawkins, F.G.S. West India Geological Survey, 1862. M.S.

(i.) Parish of St. Andrew [*With vertical sections*]. 1863. M.S.

(j.) Western Division of the Parish of Metcalfe. 1863. M.S.

(k.) Parish of St. George and part of the Parish of Metcalfe, lith. 1861.

(l.) Parish of St. George and part of the Parish of Metcalfe, [*With vertical sections.*] 1867. M.S.

(m.) Parish of St. Mary, 1863. M.S.

(n.) Parish of St. Thomas-in-the-Vale, 1863. M.S.

(o.) Parish of St. Dorothy [*With vertical sections*]. 1864. M.S.

(p.) Sections illustrating the Geological structure of the Parishes of Metcalfe, St. Mary and St. Thomas-in-the-Vale, 1863. M.S.

(q.) Parish of St. Catherine, 1864. M.S.

(r.) Parish of St. John, [*With vertical sections*]. 1864. M.S.

(s.) Parish of Vere, [*With vertical sections*]. 1864. M.S.

(t.) Parish of Manchester, 1865. M.S.

(u.) Parish of Clarendon, [*With vertical sections*]. 1865. M.S.

(v.) Parish of St. Ann, [*With vertical sections*]. 1866. M.S.

(*w.*) Parish of St. Elizabeth, 1865. M.S.
(*x.*) Sections illustrating the Geology of the Parishes of Manchester and St. Elizabeth, n.d. M.S.
(*y.*) Parish of Trelawny [*With vertical sections*]. 1866. M.S.
(*z.*) Parish of Westmoreland [*With vertical sections*]. 1866. M.S.
(*aa.*) Parish of St. James [*With vertical sections*]. 1866. M.S.
(*bb.*) Parish of Hanover [*With vertical sections*]. 1866. M.S.

1865. 51. Geological Map of Jamaica. By James G. Sawkins and Chas. B. Brown. 1865. Scale ½in. =1 mile. [*In Sawkins's " Reports on the Geology of Jamaica." 1869.*]

"   51a. *Map of the County of Surrey in the Island of Jamaica, showing its topographical features—the line of march of the Troops and Maroons, and the situation of the several villages burnt or partially so during the disturbances in October and November, 1865. Prepared for the information of the Royal Commissioners by John Parry, Esq., Engineer for the County of Surrey. M.S. Scale 1in. =1 mile.

1866. 51b. The County of Surrey, Jamaica, shewing the various marches of Troops, &c., during the late rebellion ; from information collected by Edward J. Castle, Lt. R.E. [By] J. R. Mann, Lt.-Col. and C.R.E. 25th Jany., 1866. Scale 1in. =1 mile. [*In " Jamaica Disturbances. Papers laid before the Royal Commission of Inquiry by Governor Eyre." London, 1866.*]

1867. *Parishes reduced from 22 to 14.*

"   52. Jamaica. 1867. [No scale : Island : 10½in. long. *In Harvey and Brewin's " Jamaica in 1866."*]

1873. 52a. Map of Jamaica prepared, from the best authorities under the direction of Major-General J. R. Mann, R.E., Director of Roads and Surveyor General, by Thomas Harrison, Government Surveyor, Kingston, Ja., 1873. Sale 3¾ in. = 10 miles.

1873. 53. Jamaica. 1873. [No scale. Island 8½ in. long. *In Gardner's " History of Jamaica." 1873*]

1876-1891. 53a. *Cadastral Maps of the different Parishes of the Island prepared, from numerous surveys made at different times by different surveyors, being the best authorities possible, by Thomas Harrison, Government Surveyor. [*These maps represent every property and parcel of land in the Island from 10 acres and upwards, and shew the extent, area, boundaries and names as well as the names of the owners ; also the Roads, Rivers and topographical details. In the Surveyor-General's office, Kingston.*] Scale 20 chains or a quarter of a mile = 1 inch.

(*a.*) Kingston, 1887.   (*h.*) St. James, 1889.
(*b.*) St. Andrew, 1877.   (*i.*) Hanover, 1891.
(*c.*) St. Thomas, 1881.   (*j.*) Westmoreland, 1890.
(*d.*) Portland, 1876.   (*k.*) St. Elizabeth, 1886.
(*e.*) St. Mary, 1880.   (*l.*) Manchester, 1885.
(*f.*) St. Ann, 1879.   (*m.*) Clarendon, 1883-84.
(*g.*) Trelawny, 1888.   (*n.*) St. Catherine, 1883.

1877. 54. Jamaica. The north and west Coasts compiled chiefly from a running survey by Commander R. Owen, R.N., 1831. The South Coast from the surveys of Staff Commander G. Stanley, R.N., 1873-75 ; and Lieutenant T. F. Pullen, R.N., 1876. Published at the Admiralty 31st March, 1866 ; under the superintendence of Captain G. H. Richards, R.N., Hydrographer, Corrections Nov. 1877.

1879. 54a. *The Island of Jamaica. James Wyld, Geographer to the Queen, London, 1879. Lithograph. Scale 5 miles = 1 inch.

1880, 55. Jamaica. Surveyed by Staff Commander G. Stanley, R.N., 1873-5 and Lieut. T. F. Pullen, R.N., 1876-9. Morant Cays by Lieut.

A. Carpenter and the Officers of H.M.S. " Sparrowhawk," **1880**, London.   Published at the Admiralty 27th October, 1880 ; under the superintendence of Captain F. J. Evans, R.N., C.B., F.R.S.

1883.   55a. A Map of Jamaica.   Compiled by J. J. Wood, a Government Inspector of Schools.   McCartney and Wood.   Kingston. Ja., 1883.   Scale 13 miles = 1 inch.

1884.   56. United Presbyterian Missionary Map of Jamaica, 1882.   Scale 1 inch. = 20 miles.   [*In Carlile's " Thirty-eight years Mission Life in Jamaica," 1884.*]

1885.   57. The Map of the Island of Jamaica prepared for the Jamaica Handbook under the direction of Thomas Harrison, Govt. Surveyor, by C lin Liddell.   1885.   [*This Map first appeared in " The Handbook of Jamaica" for 1886, and amended editions have appeared in subsequent editions of the book.*]

1886.   58. Map of Jamaica.   By C. Washington Eves.   1886.   Scale 1¾ in. = 10 miles.   [*In "Eves's "Jamaica at the Colonial and Indian Exhibition."*]

1888.   59. Map of Jamaica prepared from the best authorities by order of His Excellency Sir Henry Wylie Norman, G.C.B., Captain-General and Governor-in-Chief, 1888.   Prepared in the Public Works Department by Colin Liddell, Acting Government Surveyor, Kingston, Jamaica, 26th January, 1888.   Scale 5½ in = 15 miles.

1890.   60. Sugar Map of Jamaica, Showing Sugar Estates in 1790 and in 1890.   Prepared for the Institute of Jamaica by Colin Liddell 1890,   M.S.   Scale 1½ inches = 4 miles.

"   61. Hydrographic Map of Jamaica, shewing the River Basins and the Rainfall.   Prepared for the Institute of Jamaica by Colin Liddell.   1890.   M.S.   Scale 1½ inches = 4 miles.

"   62. Geological Map of Jamaica, enlarged from the Map of Sawkins and Brown for the Institute of Jamaica, by Colin Liddell.   1890. M.S.   Scale 1½ inches = 4 miles.

"   63. Map, showing the Mountain and River Systems of Jamaica, prepared for the Institute of Jamaica by Colin Liddell.   1890. M.S, Scale 1½ inches = 4 miles.

"   64. Map, showing the Extent and Distribution of Land occupied in small holdings, *i.e.*, those of 200 acres and under throughout the Island of Jamaica, prepared for the Institute of Jamaica by Colin Liddell.   1890.   M.S.   Scale 1½ inches = 4 miles.

1891.   65. Map of the Island of Jamaica.   Compiled for Aston W. Gardner & Co., Kingston, Ja. n.d. [?1891.]   Scale 4½ in. = 28 miles.

1892.   65a. The Rainfall of Jamaica.   Thirteen maps showing the average Rainfall in each month and during the year with explanatory text.   By Maxwell Hall, M.A., folio, Kingston, Ja., 1892. Scale ₁⅝ inch = 1 mile.

1894.   66. Mission Map of Jamaica [Showing the Mission Stations of The United Presbyterian Church in the Island.] 1894. Scale ¼ in.=5 miles.   [*In Robson's " The Story of our Jamaica Mission," 1894.*]

1895.   67. A Map of the Island of Jamaica prepared for " Jamaica in 1895." Scale 3 in. = 25 miles.   [*In " Jamaica in 1895." Revised editions appeared in 1896, 1897 and 1901.*]

1897.   67a. Diocesan Map of the Island of Jamaica : issued as a supplement to the " Jamaica Churchman" December, 1897.

1898.   67b. Bacon's Excelsior Map of Jamaica. By G. W. Bacon, F.R.G.S., with an inset map of the West Indies.   Scale 1 inch = 4 miles.   [1898.]

1899.   67c. Configuration of Jamaica.   Scale 5 miles = 1 inch.   [*In Hill's " Geology and Physical Geography of Jamaica." 1899.*]

"   67d. Geologic Map of Jamaica.   Compiled from Map of Sawkins and Brown with additional data by Robert T. Hill.   1898. Scale

5 miles = 1 inch. [*In Hill's "Geology and Physical Geography of Jamaica."* 1899.]

1899 67e. Tourist Map of the Island of Jamaica, B.W.I. Compiled from various authorities by E. V. d'Invilliers, Geologist and Mining Engineer. Philadelphia, Pa. 1899. Scale about $6\frac{5}{12}$ miles = 1 inch.

" Gardner's Memory Maps. Kingston, Ja. n.d.

" Geological Map of Jamaica. After Sawkins, Brown and Hill. By Alfred G. Nash, B.Sc. &c. [In *"The Scottish Geographical Magazine."* 1899.]

1900. *Port Royal divided from Kingston for purposes of civic administration.*

Plans of Towns.

Kingston and Port Royal.

1683. 68. Port Royal. Photographic copy of part of a Manuscript Map in the British Museum by G. Hack, 1683.

1733. 69. Port Royal. Facsimile of the map which accompanies Sir Hans Sloane's Account of the Port Royal Earthquake in the "Transactions of the Royal Society." [*In the "Journal of the Institute of Jamaica,"* 1893.]

" 70. Kingston Harbour in Jamaica. [*In Popple's " Map of the British Empire in America."* 1733.]

1738. 70a. A Plan of the ground at The North East End of Port Royal that will be required in case his Majesty thinks it necessary to erect any buildings there for the use of the Navy. [*In "Acts of Assembly passed in the Island of Jamaica from 1661 to 1737, London 1738.*]

1740. 70b. Kingston, capitale de la Jamaïque, bâtie par les Anglois en 1692 n. d. [1740.]

" 70c. Port Royal de Jamaïque. n. d. [1740.]

1758. 71. Plan de la Ville de Kingston, suivant le projet donné par le Colonel Christian Lilly. [*In " Description Geographique des Isles Antilles possedées par les Anglois."* Paris. 1758.]

" 72. Carte des Harves de Kingstown, et de Port Royal. [*In " Description Geographiques des Isles Antilles possedées par les Anglois."* Paris. 1758.]

1762. 72a. Plan de la ville de Port Royal, Jamaïque. [Bellin, Paris, 1762.]

" 72b. Plan de la ville de Kingston, suivant le projet donné par le Colonel Christian Lilly. [par le Sr. Bellin, Paris, 1762.]

" 72c. Carte des Havres de Kingstown, et de Port Royal. [Bellin, Paris 1762.]

1774. 73. A Draught of the Harbours of Port Royal and Kingston. 1774. [*In Long's " History of Jamaica."*]

1782. 74. A Draught of the Harbours of Port Royal and Kingston, in Jamaica, with the Fortifications correctly laid down ; also all the Keys and Shoals adjacent. Jno. Lodge, sulp. London 28th of Feby. 1782. Scale $5\frac{3}{8}$ in. = 5 miles.

1799. 75. Port Royal in Jamaica. Engraved for Luffman's " Select Plans of the principal cities, ports, harbours and forts in the world." Published July 1, 1799. London. Scale $1\frac{5}{8}$ in. = 4 miles.

1803. 76. Plan des Rades et Villes de Kingston et Port Royal, dans l'Isle de la Jamaïque, dessiné d'après celui de Don Lopez, par George de Bois St. lys, Anc. Offr. Francais, 1803. [M.S.] Scale $\frac{1}{4}$ in. = 400 Toises.

1818. 76a. Plano del Puerto de Kingston y Pto. Real.   [Madrid 1818.]
1823. 76b. *A Plan of the City of Kingston in the Island of Jamaica. Pro-
            tracted from the Original Surveys of Lilly, Sheriff and Munro
            and P. H. Keiffe. 1823. [By David Smith]. No scale.
1843. 77. A Plan of the City of Kingston, shewing the dreadful conflagra-
            tion on the 26–27 of August, 1843. Description. Kingston as laid
            down by C. Lilly in 1693, extending from West Street to Fleet
            Street but only to Rum Lane above it. Lithographed by G.
            Muguet. Scale 1¾ in. = 1,000 feet.
1848. 78. Kidd's New Plan of the City of Kingston. Lithographed for
            and published by A. deCordova and Nephew. [n.d.ab. 1848.]
1872. 78a. *Plan of the city of Kingston in sheets. Scale 88 feet = 1 inch.
            [Prepared about 1872.] [M.S. in Public Works Office].
1889. 79. Plan of the City of Kingston and its suburbs prepared for Aston
            W. Gardner & Co. London 1889. Scale 1 in. = 600 feet.
1891. 79a. Kingston Jamaica. Rough sketch of country round Kingston,
            Jamaica, compiled from Maps, and corrected by reference to the
            Admiralty Charts. Sketches by T. Harrison; Captain Wood-
            ford, York and Lancashire Regiment; Capt. Thwaytes, Lieut.
            Phillips and Lieut. Climo, W. India Regiment, and personal
            observation by Major C. E. de la Poer Beresford, D.A.A.G.
            Published on behalf of the War Office. London, 1891.
1892–97. 79b. *Map of the City of Kingston in sheets. Scale 10ft. = 1 inch.
            Prepared 1892–1897 for the Kingston Improvement Commis-
            sioners. [M.S. in Commissioner's Office].
1896. 79c. *Plan of the Town of Port Royal, Jamaica, made by an order of
            the Magistrates and Vestry, dated 16th November, 1896. By
            Archibald Turnbull, Surveyor. M.S. 100ft. = 1 in.
1898. 79d. Kingston and Surrounding district. Reduced from a sketch
            drawn on a scale of 4 inches to one mile by Captains B. F.
            Stevens and J. S. Henderson. 1st W. India Regiment. War
            Office, London, 1898. Scale 1 in. = 1 mile.
                [See also Nos. 1ʼ, 15-18, 27-30, 32, 33, 36, 43.]

MORANT BAY.

1818. 79d. Plano del Pto. Morante. [Madrid 1818.]

PORT MORANT.

1792. 79e. A Plan of Port Morant, Jamaica. Drawn from Leard's Survey
            taken in 1792. [Manuscript.]

PORT ANTONIO.

       80. Plan des Harves de Port Antonio et de Saint Francois, situés à
            la coste du Nord Est de l'Isle de la Jamaïque. n.d. Scale 1 in.
            = 300 Toises.
       81. Puerto Antonio, Jamayca. n d.
1733. 82. A plan of the Harbour of Port Antonio in Jamaica. [In Popple's
            "Map of the British Empire in Jamaica." 1733.]
1762. 82a. Plan des Havres de Port Antonio et de Saint Francois situés à
            la coste du N.E. de la Jamaïque. [Bellin. Paris, 1762.]
1774. 83. Plan of the Harbours of Port Antonio in the Island of Jamaica,
            survey'd A.D. 1771. Engraved by T. Kitchin. 1774. [In Long's
            "History of Jamaica"].
1788. 84. The Harbours of Port Antonio in Jamaica. London. Printed
            for Robert Sayer, June 1. 1788.
       85. The Harbours of Port Antonio in Jamaica. London. Jany. 1st
            1788.
1795. 85a. *A Plan of the Town of Titchfield [now Port Antonio]. Per-
            formed by order of the Vestry, June, 1795, by David Cowan.
            [MS. in the Surveyor General's Office]. Scale 200 feet = 1 inch.
                [See also No. 16.]

St. Ann's Bay.

1818.   85aa. Bahia de Sta Ana.   [Madrid 1818.]

Lucea and Montego Bay.

1788.   85b. Plan of Lucia Harbour and Montego Bay in Jamaica.   London, Robert Sayer.   1788.

1818.   85bb. Bahia de Lucea.   (Madrid 1818.]

   "   85c. Bahia de Montego.   [Madrid 1818.]

1825.   85cc. *Plan of the Town of Montega Bay. No date ; supposed to be by Morris and Cunningham, Surveyors, some time in 1825. Scale 100 feet = 1 inch.   [*M.S. in Public Works Office.*]

Mosquito Cove.

1818.   85cc. Puerto de Mosquito.   [Madrid 1818.]

Savanna-la-Mar.

1889.   86. *Plan of the Town of Savanna-la-Mar and suburbs. Surveyed in 1889 by Thomas Harrison, Surveyor-General.   Scale 5 chains = 1 in.   M.S.   [*In Surveyor General's Office*].

Bluefields.

1818.   86a.   Plan del Fondeadero de Bluefields.   [Madrid 1818.]
                        [*See also* No. 30, 32, 36, 43.]

Southern Jamaica.

1682.   87. Southern Jamaica.   Photographic copy of Part of a Map in the British Museum by Gulielmus Hack.   1682.

St. Jago de la Vega.

88. Plan of the Town of St. Jago de la Vega, Jamaica, David Soares, Town-warden.   A Duperly, lith.   [n.d.] Scale 1 in. = five chains.

Cock Pits.

1803.   89. Map of the Interior Part of Jamaica called the Cock Pits, which was the seat of the Maroon War in 1795 and 1796.   Drawn by J. Robertson, Esq., A.M., whose new maps of that Island are now engraving, Jan. 1st. 1803.   [*In Dallas's " History of the Maroons."*]

Turks Islands.

1775.   90. Turks Islands, from a survey made in 1753, by the sloops l'Aigle and l'Emerande, by order of the French Governor of Hispaniola, with improvements from observations made in 1770, in the Sr. Edward Hawke, King's Schooner.   London 20 Feb.   1775. Scale 1½ in. = 1 mile.

1810.   91. Turks Islands.   From a survey made by the Sloops l'Aigle and l'Emerande, by order of the French Governor of Hispaniola, with improvements from observations recently made by English and Spanish Officers.   London.   12 Sep. 1810.